Japanese
phrase book

PERIPLUS

Published in 2000 by Periplus Editions (HK) Ltd.

LCC Card No. 99-066975
ISBN: 962-593-804-4

Distributed by:

North America
Tuttle Publishing
Airport Industrial Park
364 Innovation Park
North Clarendon, VT 05759-9436
Tel: (802) 773 8930; Fax: (802) 773 6993

Japan & Korea
Tuttle Publishing
RK Building, 2nd Floor
2-13-10 Shimo-Meguro, Meguro-ku
Tokyo 153 0064
Tel: (03) 5437 0171; Fax: (03) 5437 0755

Asia Pacific
Berkeley Books Pte. Ltd.
130 Joo Seng Road, #06-01/03
Singapore 368357
Tel: (65) 6 280 1330; Fax: (65) 6 280 6290

First edition
07 06 05 04 03 02   10 9 8 7 6 5 4 3

Printed in Singapore

Contents

Introduction

● **Welcome to the Periplus new Essential Phrase Books series, covering the world's most popular languages and containing everything you'd expect from a comprehensive language series. They're concise, accessible and easy to understand, and you'll find them indispensable on your trip abroad.**

Each guide is divided into 15 themed sections and starts with a pronunciation table which explains the phonetic pronunciation to all the words and phrases you'll need to know for your trip, while at the back of the book is an extensive word list and grammar guide which will help you construct basic sentences in your chosen language.

Throughout the book you'll come across colored boxes with a 🥢 beside them. These are designed to help you if you can't understand what your listener is saying to you. Hand the book over to them and encourage them to point to the appropriate answer to the question you are asking.

Other colored boxes in the book – this time without the symbol – give alphabetical listings of themed words with their English translations beside them.

For extra clarity, we have put all English words and phrases in black, foreign language terms in red and their phonetic pronunciation in italic.

This phrase book covers all subjects you are likely to come across during the course of your visit, from reserving a room for the night to ordering food and drink at a restaurant and what to do if your car breaks down or you lose your traveler's checks and money. With over 2,000 commonly used words and essential phrases at your fingertips you can rest assured that you will be able to get by in all situations, so let the Essential Phrase Book become your passport to a secure and enjoyable trip!

Pronunciation table

Japanese is very easy to pronounce. It is made up of strings of syllables (a, ka, ta, etc.) which just join together following very simple rules of pronunciation (e.g. anata is *a-na-ta*). Unlike English, each syllable has mostly even stress and combinations of vowels (e-i, a-i, etc.) do not represent completely new sounds.

Vowels

Japanese has five vowels, pronounced either long or short. Distinguishing the length is very important as sometimes the meaning depends on the difference (e.g. ojisan/ojiisan, terms of address to a middle-aged man and an old man respectively). Note that a final e is always pronounced (e.g. sake, rice wine, is pronounced close to *sakay*).

a	like **a** in America	*a*	**asa**	*asa*
ā	**ah** (as in the exclamation !)	*ah*	**mā**	*mah*
e	**e** as in pet or	*e*	**desu**	*des*
	ay is in sway, but shorter	*ay*	**sake**	*sakay*
ē	**eh** sounded long, like **ere** in there	*eh*	**eetone**	*eh-to-nay*
i	like **i** in pit, though slightly longer	*i*	**nichi**	*nichi*
ī	**ee** as in keep	*ee*	**iie**	*ee-ye*
o	**o** as in top	*o*	**yoru**	*yoru*
ō	**ou** as in four	*oh*	**kyō**	*kyoh*
u	**u** as in put	*u*	**haru**	*haru*
ū	**oo** as in coop	*oo*	**chūmon**	*choomon*

Consonants

Most consonants are pronounced in a similar manner to English.

b	**b** as in bat	*b*	**bin**	*bin*
ch	**ch** as in chip	*ch*	**nichi**	*nichi*
d	**d** as in day	*d*	**dame**	*damay*
f	**f** as in food	*f*	**fuyu**	*fu-yu*
g	**g** as in give	*g*	**gogo**	*gogo*
h	**h** as in hat	*h*	**haru**	*haru*
j	**j** as in jump	*j*	**niji**	*niji*
k	**k** as in king	*k*	**koko**	*koko*
m	**m** as in mat	*m*	**totemo**	*totemo*
n	**n** as in nut.	*n*	**namae**	*nama-e*
	at the end of a word			
	may be more like **ng**	*n (g)*	**yen**	*yen (g)*
	ng as in thing	*ng*	**ringo**	*ring-o*
p	**p** as in pat	*p*	**posuto**	*pos-to*
r	Somewhere between English **r**, **l** and **d**. Never rolled **r**; more like **r** in car	*r*	**raigetsu**	*righ-gets*
s	**s** as in start	*s*	**semete**	*semetay*
sh	**sh** as in ship	*sh*	**shio**	*shi-o*
t	**t** as in tip	*t*	**dōshite**	*doh-shtay*
ts	**ts** as in hits	*ts*	**itsu**	*its*
w	**w** as in watt	*w*	**wakaru**	*wakaru*
y	**y** as in yes	*y*	**yoru**	*yoru*
z	**z** as in zoo	*z*	**mizu**	*mizu*

Note: when **i** and **u** follow **k, s, t, h, p** or come between two of them, they become very shortened and are often not heard at all (e.g. **desu** becomes *des* and **mimashita** becomes *mimashta*).

Vowel combinations

Basically, each vowel should be pronounced separately. The most common combinations are:

ai	**igh** as in high	*igh*	**hai**	*high*
ao	**ow** as in now	*ow*	**nao**	*now*
ei	**ay** as in play	*ay*	**rei**	*ray*
ue	**weigh** as in weight	*eigh*	**ue**	*weigh*

Useful lists

Useful lists

.1 Today or tomorrow?

What day is it today?	今日は何曜日ですか。
	kyoh-wa nan-yohbi des-ka
Today's Monday	今日は月曜日です。
	kyoh-wa gets-yohbi des
– Tuesday	今日は火曜日です。
	kyoh-wa ka-yohbi des
– Wednesday	今日は水曜日です。
	kyoh-wa swee-yohbi des
– Thursday	今日は木曜日です。
	kyoh-wa moku-yohbi des
– Friday	今日は金曜日です。
	kyoh-wa kin-yohbi des
– Saturday	今日は土曜日です。
	kyoh-wa do-yohbi des
– Sunday	今日は日曜日です。
	kyoh-wa nichi-yohbi des
in January	一月に
	ichi-gatsu-ni
since February	二月から
	ni-gatsu-kara
in spring	春に
	haru-ni
in summer	夏に
	natsu-ni
in autumn	秋に
	aki-ni
in winter	冬に
	fuyu-ni
1999	1999年
	sen-kyoo-hyaku-kyoo-joo-hachi-nen
the twentieth century	20世紀
	nijoo-say-ki
the twenty-first century	21世紀
	nijoo-i-say-ki
What's the date today?	今日は何日ですか。
	kyoh-wa nan-nichi des-ka
Today's the 24th	今日は24日です。
	kyoh-wa nijoo-yokka des
Monday 3 November 1999	1999年11月3日の月曜日
	sen-kyoo-hyaku-kyoo-joo-hachi-nen joo-ichi-gatsu mikka no gets-yohbi
in the morning	朝に
	asa-ni
in the afternoon	午後に
	gogo-ni
in the evening	夕方に
	yoogata-ni
at night	夜に
	yoru-ni
this morning	今朝
	kesa

this afternoon	今日の午後
	kyoh no gogo
this evening	今日の夕方
	kyoh no yoogata
tonight	今晩
	kom-ban
last night	昨晩
	saku-ban
this week	今週
	kon-shoo
next month	来月
	righ-gets
last year	去年
	kyo-nen
next...	次の
	tsugi-no
in...days/weeks/ months/years	…日／週間／か月／年間に
	... nichi/shookan/ka-getsu/nenkan-ni
...weeks ago	…週間前に
	... shookan ma-e-ni
day off	休日
	kyoo-jitsu

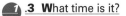 **.2** **L**egal Holidays

New Year's Day (January 1)	gan-jitsu
Adult's Day (January 15)	sayjin-no-hi
National Foundation Day (February 11)	ken-koku ki-nen-bi
Vernal Equinox Day (March 21)	shun-bun-no-hi
Greenery Day (April 29)	midori-no-hi
Constitution Day (May 3)	kempoh ki-nen-bi
Public Holiday (May 4)	kokumin-no-kyoo-jitsu
Children's Day (May 5)	kodomo-no-hi
Marine Day (July 20)	umi-no-hi
Respect for the Aged Day (September 15)	kayroh-no-hi
Autumnal Equinox Day (September 23)	shoobun-no-hi
Health-Sports Day (October 10)	tigh-iku-no-hi
Culture Day (November 3)	bunka-no-hi
Thanksgiving Day (November 23)	kinroh-kansha-no-hi
Emperor's Birthday (December 23)	tennoh tanjoh-bi

Though officially only January 1 is a public holiday during the New Year period, most banks and businesses remain shut until at least January 3. The period between April 29 and May 5 is known as Golden Week.

The Obon festival, when families return to ancestral homes to venerate the returning spirits of their ancestors, is held in country districts around mid July and in Tokyo in mid August. It should also be noted that Christmas Day is a normal business day.

.3 **W**hat time is it?

What time is it?	何時ですか。
	nanji des-ka
It's nine o'clock	（午前）9時です。
	(gozen) ku-ji des
– five past ten	（午前）10時5分…
	(gozen) joo-ji go-fun...

– a quarter past eleven _____	（午前）11時15分… *(gozen) joo-ichi-ji joo-go-fun...*
– twenty past twelve_____	（午後）12時20分… *(gogo) joo-ni-ji ni-juppun...*
– half past one _____	（午後）1時半… *(gogo) ichi-ji han...*
– twenty-five to three _____	（午後）2時35分… *(gogo) ni-ji san-joo-go-fun...*
– a quarter to four _____	（午後）3時45分… *(gogo) san-ji yon-joo-go-fun...*
– ten to five _____	（午後）4時50分… *(gogo) yo-ji go-juppun...*
– twelve noon_____	12時／正午… *joo-ni-ji/shoh-go...*
– midnight _____	夜中の12時… *yo-naka no joo-ni-ji...*
half an hour _____	三十分間 *san-juppun-kan*
What time? _____	何時？ *nanji*
What time can I come _____ by?	何時に来れば いいですか。 *nanji-ni kureba ee des-ka*
At... _____	…に *... ni*
After... _____	…過ぎに *... sugi-ni*
Before... _____	…前に *... ma-e-ni*
Between...and... _____	…と…の間に *... to ... no ai-da-ni...*
From...to... _____	…から…まで *... kara ... maday*
In...minutes _____	…分後に *... fun go-ni*
– an hour _____	1時間後に *... ichi-jikan go-ni*
– ...hours _____	…時間後に *... jikan go-ni*
– a quarter of an hour _____	15分後に *joo-go-fun go-ni*
– three quarters of _____ an hour	45分後に *yon-joo-go-fun go-ni*
early/late _____	早過ぎます／遅過ぎます。 *haya-sugi-mas/oso-sugi-mas*
on time_____	間に合って／…に間に合います。 *mani-attay/... ni mani-a-imas*

1 .4 One, two, three...

Numbers are rarely used on their own, but join with 'counters'. The counter can be joined after any of the numbers in the list below. For example, the counter for books is satsu, so that 'one book' is /is-satsu/, 'two books' is /ni-satsu/, etc.

Some of the most common counters are:

時 *ji (hour): ichi-ji (1 o'clock), ni-ji (2 o'clock)*
時間 *jikan (hours): ichi-jikan (1 hour), ni-jikan (two hours)*

枚 *mai (used for flat objects like sheets of paper): ichi-migh, ni-migh, etc.*
円 *yen (the Japanese currency): hyaku-en (100 yen), sen(g)-en (1000 yen)*
台 *dai (for machines like cars and bikes): ichi-digh, ni-digh, etc.*
杯 *hai (cups): koh-hee ni-high (two cups of coffee), o-cha go-high (five cups of tea)*
本 *hon (for cylindrical objects, like chopsticks, cigarettes, etc.): ip-pon, ni-hon, sam-bon*
人 *nin (people): san-nin (three people), roku-nin (six people). The words for one and two people are different: hi-to-ri (one person) and fu-ta-ri (two people).*

However you can avoid using counters for the numbers one to ten by employing the alternative Japanese numbering system.They are shown in brackets in the list. For example, *hambahga mits kuda-sigh* is "Two hamburgers, please."

0	_____	ray/zero
1	_____	ichi (hi-tots)
2	_____	ni (fu-tats)
3	_____	san (mits)
4	_____	shi/yon (yots)
5	_____	go (i-tsuts)
6	_____	roku (muts)
7	_____	shichi/nana (na-nats)
8	_____	hachi (yats)
9	_____	ku/kyoo (koko-nots)
10	_____	joo/ju (toh)
11	_____	joo-ichi
12	_____	joo-ni
13	_____	joo-san
14	_____	joo-shi
15	_____	joo-go
16	_____	joo-roku
17	_____	joo-shichi
18	_____	joo-hachi
19	_____	joo-ku
20	_____	ni-joo
21	_____	ni-joo-ichi
22	_____	ni-joo-ni
30	_____	san-joo
31	_____	san-joo-ichi
32	_____	san-joo-ni
40	_____	yon-joo
50	_____	go-joo
60	_____	roku-joo
70	_____	nana-joo
80	_____	hachi-joo
90	_____	kyoo-joo
100	_____	hyaku
101	_____	hyaku ichi
110	_____	hyaku joo
120	_____	hyaku ni-joo
200	_____	ni-hyaku
300	_____	sam-byaku
400	_____	yon-hyaku

500 _____	*go-hyaku*
600 _____	*rop-pyaku*
700 _____	*nana-hyaku*
800 _____	*hap-pyaku*
900 _____	*kyoo-hyaku*
1000 _____	*sen/issen*
1100 _____	*sen hyaku*
2000 _____	*ni-sen*
3000 _____	*san-zen*
8000 _____	*has-sen*
10,000 _____	*ichi-man*
20,000 _____	*ni-man*
100,000 _____	*joo-man*
a million _____	*hyaku-man*
one hundred million ____	*oku*

1st _____	第一
	dai-ichi
2nd _____	第二
	dai-ni
3rd _____	第三
	dai-san
once _____	一倍
	ichi-bigh
twice _____	二倍
	ni-bigh
triple _____	三倍
	sam-bigh
half _____	半分
	ham-bun
a quarter _____	四分の一
	yon-bun no ichi
a third _____	三分の一
	sam-bun no ichi
a couple, a few, some ____	いくつかの／二、三
	iku-tsu ka no/ ni, san
2 + 4 = 6 _____	2プラス4は6
	ni puras yon wa roku
4 – 2 = 2 _____	4マイナス2は2
	yon mighnas ni wa ni
2 x 4 = 8 _____	2かける4は8
	ni kakeru yon wa hachi
4 ÷ 2 = 2 _____	4割る2は2
	yon waru ni wa ni
odd/even _____	偶数の／奇数の
	goo-soo no/ ki-soo no
total _____	全部（で）
	zem-bu (de)
6 x 9 _____	長さは9メートル幅は6メートルです。
	nagasa wa kyoo meh-toru haba wa roku meh-toru

1.5 The weather

Is the weather going to be good/bad?	いい／悪い天気になりますか。
Is it going to get colder/hotter?	寒く／暑くなりますか。
What temperature is it going to be?	気温は何度ぐらいでしょうか。
Is it going to rain?	雨になりますか。
Is there going to be a storm?	嵐になりますか。
Is it going to snow?	雪になりますか。
Is it going to freeze?	氷が張りますか。
Is the thaw setting in?	氷が溶けるぐらいの暖かさですか。
Is it going to be foggy?	霧が立ちますか。
Is there going to be a thunderstorm?	雷雨になりますか。
The weather's changing	天気がくずれます。
It's cooling down	涼しくなります。
What's the weather going to be like today/ tomorrow?	今日／明日の天気予報はどうですか。

薄ら寒い chilly	酷暑 heat wave	嵐 stormy
快晴 clear	暑い hot	日当りのよい sunny
曇／くもり cloudy	台風 typhoon	雷雨 thunderstorm
寒い cold	穏やか mild	雨天 wet
湿っぽい damp	蒸し暑い muggy	風 wind
(氷点下) …度 ...degrees (above/ below zero)	どんよりした overcast	かすかな／強い風 light/moderate/ strong wind
霧雨 drizzle	雨 rain	風のある windy
いい天気 fine	猛暑 scorching hot	霰 sleet
霧 fog	にわか雨 shower	梅雨 rainy season
霜 frost	雪 snow	暖かい warm
ひょう hail	はやて squalls	

Useful lists

See also 5.1 Asking for directions

here/there	ここ…そこ…あそこ
	koko/soko/a-soko
somewhere	どこか
	doko-ka
nowhere	どこにも…ない
	doko ni mo...nai
everywhere	どこにでも
	doko ni demo
far away/nearby	遠い…近い
	toh-i/chi-kigh
right/left	右の方に…左の方に
	migi no hoh ni/hidari no hoh ni
to the right/left of	…の右に／…の左に
	... no migi ni/... no hidari ni
straight ahead	真っ直ぐ
	mas-sugu
via	…経由で
	... kay-yu de
in	…の中に
	... no naka ni
on	…の上に
	... no u-e ni
under	…の下に
	... no shta ni
against	…に対して
	... ni tigh-shtay
opposite	…の向こう側に
	... no mukoh-gawa ni
next to	…の隣に
	... no tonari ni
near	…の側に
	... no soba ni
in front of	…の前に
	... no ma-e ni
in the center	…の真ん中に
	... no man-naka ni
forward	前へ
	ma-e ay
down	下へ
	shta ay
up	上へ
	u-e ay
inside	中へ
	naka ay
outside	外へ
	soto ay
behind	後へ
	ushiro ay
at the front	前に
	ma-e ni
at the back	後に
	ushiro ni

in the north	北の方に	*kita no hoh ni*
to the south	南の方へ	*minami no hoh ni*
from the west	西の方から	*nishi no hoh kara*
from the east	東の方から	*hi-gashi no hoh kara*

.7 What does that sign say?

危険 danger	案内 information	銀行 bank
注意 warning	観光案内所 tourist information	警察署 police station
応急手当 first aid	受付け reception	窓口 counter
緊急ブレーキ／非常 ブレーキ emergency brake	満員 full	切符 tickets
避難階段 fire escape	営業中 open	待合室 waiting room
緊急出口／非常口 emergency exit	準備中 closed	停留所／バス停 bus stop
通行禁止 no thoroughfare	押／引 push/pull	停車場／タクシー 乗り場 taxi stand
入場無料 no charge	故障中 out of order	郵便箱／ポスト post box
禁煙 no smoking	予約済 reserved	〒 mail
喫煙 smoking	支払い所 pay here	猛犬注意 beware of the dog
手をふれないで ください。 please do not touch	売出し sale/clearance	火気厳禁 no open fires
ペンキ塗りたて wet paint	売り物 for sale	高圧注意 high voltage
芝生に入らないで 下さい。 keep off the grass	階段 stairs	足下注意 watch your step
撮影禁止 no photographs	エスカレーター escalator	立入禁止 no entry
起こさないで ください。 do not disturb	エレベーター elevator	ペット禁止 no pets allowed
入口 entrance	階 ...floor	営業時間 opening hours
出口 exit	トイレ／お手洗い／ 便所（女性／男性） toilets/gents/ gentlemen/ladies	私有地 private (property)

🔵 .8 Personal details

In Japan the family name comes first and the given name next. Titles come after the name. The title -san can be attached either to the surname or the given name, and is used for both males and females, being the equivalent of Mr, Mrs and Miss. Small children are addressed by their given name plus -chan, and boys by either their given name (among friends) or their surname (at school, for example) plus -kun. Superiors may also address subordinates in companies by their surname plus -kun. Anyone regarded as an intellectual is called sensei (sen-say, 'teacher').

your name_____	お名前 *onama-e*
my name _____	名前 *nama-e*
surname_____	名字（苗字）／姓 *myohji/say*
given name(s) _____	名前 *nama-e*
address_____	住所 *joo-sho*
postal/zip code _____	郵便番号 *yoobin bango*
sex (male/female) _____	性（男／女） *say (dan/jo)*
nationality _____	国籍 *koku-seki*
date of birth _____	生年月日 *say-nen-gappi*
place of birth_____	出生地 *shushoh-chi*
occupation_____	職業 *shoku-gyoh*
married/single/divorced____	既婚／未婚／離婚 *ki-kon/mi-kon/ri-kon*
(number of) children_____	子供（の数） *ko-domo (no kazu)*
passport/identity card/ _____ driving license number	パスポート（旅券）／身分証明書／ 運転免許書の番号 *pasu-pohto (ryo-ken)/mibun shoh-may-sho/* *unten men-kyo-sho no bango*

Courtesies

2 Courtesies

The use of courtesies is considered important in Japan. When someone does something for you, a simple *dohmo sumimasen* (thank you for your trouble) is greatly appreciated. On meeting, the Japanese greet each other with a bow from the waist, of varying depth. Non-Japanese need not do so, though this is a custom which people find themselves following almost unconsciously after a short time. Men in particular may greet a European with a handshake. It is of utmost importance that shoes are taken off when entering private homes. There is a greater tolerance of proximity in Japan than in the U.S.; in trains, elevators and other crowded public places, physical contact is unavoidable. It is polite, however, to maintain a kind of mental privacy. Impatience is rarely shown in public, while displays of anger cause embarrassment and are rarely effective.

2 .1 Greetings

Good morning	おはよう（ございます）。 *o-high-yoh (goza-i-masu)*
Hello	こんにちは。 *kon-nichi wa*
Good evening	今晩は。 *kom-ban wa*
Good afternoon	今日は。 *kon-nichi wa*
How are you?	お元気ですか。 *o-genki des-ka*
Fine, thank you, and you?	はい、元気です。あなたは？ *high, genki des. anata wa*
Very well	おかげさまで。 *o-kagay-sama day*
Not too bad	まあまあです。 *mah mah des*
I'd better be going	じゃあ、失礼します。 *jah, shi-tsu-ray shimas*
I have to be going. Someone's waiting for me	人を待たせていますので、 これで失礼いたします。 *shto-o matasetay imas no day,* *koray-de shi-tsu-ray itashimas*
Good bye	さよなら。 *sayoh-nara*
See you soon	またあとで。 *mata ato-day*
Good night	お休みなさい。 *oyasumi nasa-i*
Good evening	今晩は。 *kom-ban wa*
Good luck	がんばって下さい。 *gambattay kuda-sigh*
Have fun	楽しんで下さい。 *tano-shinday kuda-sigh*
Look after yourself	ごきげんよう！ *gokigen-yoh*
Have a nice vacation	楽しい休暇を。 *tanoshee kyookay-o*

Have a good trip _____	楽しい旅行を。
	tanoshee ryokoh-o
Thank you, you too_____	どうもありがとう。あなたも。
	dohmo arigatoh, anata-mo
Say hello to...for me _____	…によろしく。
	... ni yoroshku

2 .2 How to ask a question

Who?_____	誰？
	daray
Who's that?_____	誰ですか。
	daray des-ka
What? _____	何？
	nani
What's there to _____ see here?	この近くで何か面白いことがありますか。
	kono chikaku day nani-ka omoshiroi
	koto-ga arimas-ka
What kind of hotel _____ is that?	どんなホテルですか。
	donna hoteru des-ka
Where?_____	どこ？
	doko
Where's the bathroom?____	トイレはどこにありますか。
	toiray-wa doko-ni arimas-ka
Where are you going? _____	どちらに行かれますか。
	dochira-ni ikaremas-ka
Where are you from? _____	どこから来ましたか。
	doko-kara kimashta-ka
How?_____	どう？
	doh
How far is that? _____	どのくらい遠いですか。
	dono kurigh toh-i des-ka
How long does that take? _	何時間かかりますか。
	nan-jikan kakarimas-ka
How long is the trip? _____	旅行はどのくらいかかりますか。
	ryokoh-wa dono kurigh kakarimas-ka
How much?_____	いくらですか。
	ikura des-ka
How many?_____	いくつですか。
	ikutsu des-ka
How much is this?_____	これはいくらですか。
	koray-wa ikura des-ka
What time is it? _____	今何時ですか。
	ima nanji des-ka
Which....? _____	どの…？
	dono...
Which? _____	どれ？
	doray...
Which glass is mine? _____	どのコップが私のですか。
	dono koppu-ga watashi-no des-ka
When? _____	いつ？
	itsu
When are you leaving? ____	いつ出ますか。
	itsu demas-ka
Why?_____	どうして／なぜ
	dohshtay / nazay

19

Could you help me, _____ please?	手伝って下さいませんか。 *tetsudattay kudasa-i-masen-ka*
Could you point that_____ out to me?	教えて下さいませんか。 *oshietay kudasa-i-masen-ka*
Could you come _____ with me, please?	連れていって下さいませんか。 *tsuretay ittay kudasa-i-masen-ka*
Could you reserve some __ tickets for me, please?	予約していただけますか。 *yoyaku shitay itadakemas-ka*
Do you know...? _____	… （を）知っていますか。 *... (o) shtte imas-ka*
Do you know another _____ hotel, please?	他のホテルを紹介して下さい。 *hoka-no hoteru-o shohkaigh shtay kuda-sigh*
Do you have a...?_____	… （が）ありますか。 *... (ga) arimas-ka*
Do you have a _____ vegetarian dish, please?	ベジタリアン料理はありますか。 *bejitarian-ryohri-wa arimas-ka*
I'd like... _____	…お願いします。 *... onega-i-shimas*
I'd like a kilo of apples, ____ please	リンゴを一キロ下さい。 *ringo-o ikkiro kuda-sigh*
Can I take this?_____	これを持って行ってもいいですか。 *kore-o mottay ittay-mo ee des-ka*
Can I smoke here? _____	タバコを吸ってもいいですか。 *tabako-o suttay-mo ee des-ka*
Could I ask you _____ something?	すみませんが *sumimasen-nga*

2 .3 How to reply

Yes, of course_____	はい、もちろん。 *high, mochiron*
No, I'm sorry_____	いいえ、すみません。 *ee-ye, sumimasen*
Yes, what can I do _____ for you?	はい、どうぞ。 *high, dohzo*
Just a moment, please ____	ちょっと待って下さい。 *chotto mattay kudasa-i*
No, I don't have _____ time now	すみませんが、時間がありません。 *sumimasen-nga, jikan-nga arimasen*
No, that's impossible _____	不可能です。 *fukanoh des*
I think so _____	そう思います。 *soh omo-imas*
No, no one _____	誰もいません。 *dare-mo imasen*
No, nothing_____	何もありません。 *nani-mo arimasen*
That's right _____	それで結構です。 *soray-day kekkoh des*
That's different_____	違います。 *chiga-i-masu*
I agree_____	賛成です。 *sansay des*
I don't agree _____	賛成出来ません。 *sansay dekimasen*
All right _____	いいです。 *ee des*

Okay	いいですよ
	ee des-yo
Perhaps	多分
	tabun
I don't know	わかりません/知りません
	wakarimasen/shirimasen

2.4 Thank you

Thank you	（どうも）ありがとう。
	(dohmo) arigatoh
You're welcome	どういたしまして。
	doh itashi-mashtay
Thank you very much	どうもありがとうございます。
	dohmo arigatoh goza-i-mas
Very kind of you	ご親切に！
	go-shinsetsu-ni
I enjoyed it very much	本当に楽しかったです。
	hontoh-ni tanoshikatta des
Thank you for your trouble	どうもありがとうございました
	dohmo arigatoh goza-i-mashta
You shouldn't have	すみませんでした。
	sumimasen deshta
That's all right	どういたしまして。
	doh itashimashtay

2.5 Sorry

Excuse me	すみません
	sumimasen
I'm sorry, I didn't know...	…知らなかったので、申し訳ありません。
	... shiranakatta no-day, mohshi-wakay-arimasen
I do apologize	すみませんでした。
	sumimasen deshta
I'm sorry	申し訳ありません。
	mohshi-wakay-arimasen
I didn't do it on purpose, it was an accident	わざとやったわけではないので、お許し下さい。
	waza-to yatta wakay de-wa-nai no-day, oyurushi-kuda-sigh
That's all right	いいですよ
	ee des-yo
Never mind	まあまあ
	mah mah
It could've happened to anyone	それは誰にでも起こりえることです。
	soray-wa daray-ni demo okori-eru koto des

2.6 What do you think?

Which do you prefer?	どちらがお好きですか。
	dochira-ga o-ski des-ka
What do you think?	どう思いますか。
	doh omoimas-ka
Don't you like dancing?	踊るのが嫌いですか。
	odoru no-ga ki-righ des-ka
I don't mind	何でもいいです。
	nandemo ee des

Well done! _____	よかった。
	yokatta
Not bad! _____	それほど悪くない！
	soray hodo waruku-nai
Great! _____	すばらしい！
	subarashee
Wonderful food! _____	おいしい！
	oi-shee
It's really nice here! _____	楽しいですねえ！
	tanoshee des-ne
How nice! _____	すてき！
	steki
How pretty! _____	きれい！
	kiray
How nice for you! _____	いいですね。
	ee des-ne
I'm very happy with... _____	…に満足しています。
	... ni manzoku shitay imas
I'm not very happy _____ with...	…に満足していません。 *... ni manzoku shitay imasen*
I'm glad... _____	…うれしい。
	... ureshee
I'm having a great time ____	とても楽しんでいます。
	totemo tanoshinde imas
I'm looking forward to it ___	それを楽しみに待っています。
	soray-o tanoshimi-ni mattay-imas
That's great_____	すごい！
	sugoi
What a pity! _____	残念！
	zannen
That's ridiculous!_____	ばかばかしい！
	baka-baka-shee
What nonsense/How silly! _	ばからしい！
	bakara-shee
I don't like... _____	…は嫌いです。
	... wa ki-righ des
I'm bored to death _____	うんざりだよ。
	unzari da-yo
I've had enough_____	もうあきた。
	moh akita
This is no good _____	だめ（だ）よ。
	damay (da) yo

Conversation

Conversation

.1 I beg your pardon?

I don't speak any _____	ぜんぜん話せません。 *zen-zen ha-nase-masen*
I speak a little... _____	少しだけ…話せます。 *skoshi dakay ... ha-nasay-mas*
I'm American _____	私はアメリカ人です。 *Watashi-wa Amerika-jin des*
Do you speak English?____	英語は話せますか。 *Aygo/-wa hanasay-mas-ka*
Is there anyone who _____ speaks...?	ここには…が話せる人がいますか。 *koko ni-wa ... ga hanaseru shto-ga imas-ka*
I beg your pardon? _____	何とおっしゃいましたか。 *nan-to ossha-i-mashta-ka*
I understand _____	分かりました。 *wakarimashta*
I don't understand_____	ちょっと分かりませんが。 *chotto wakarimasen-nga*
Do you understand me? ___	分かりますか。 *wakarimas-ka*
Could you repeat that, ____ please?	もう一度言って下さい。 *moh ichido ittay kuda-sigh*
Could you speak more ____ slowly, please?	ゆっくり話して下さいませんか。 *yukkuri hanashtay kudasai-masen-ka*
What does that mean?____	それはどういう意味ですか。 *soray-wa doh yoo imi des-ka*
What does that word _____ mean?	その言葉はどういう意味ですか。 *sono kotoba-wa doh yoo imi des-ka*
Is that similar to/ _____ the same as...?	それは…という意味ですか。 *soray-wa... to yoo imi des-ka*
Could you write that _____ down for me, please?	それを書いて下さいませんか。 *soray-o kaitay kudasa-i-masen-ka*
Could you point that _____ out in this phrase book, please?	この本の中でそれを指さして下さいませんか。 *kono hon-no naka-de sore-o yubi-sashtay kudasa-i-masen-ka*
One moment, please, I ___ have to look it up	ちょっと待って下さい、捜してみます。 *chotto mattay kudasa-i, sagashtay mimas*
I can't find the word _____	言葉が見つかりません。 *kotoba-ga mitsukarimasen*
How do you say _____ that in Japanese?	それは日本語でどう言いますか。 *soray-wa nihongo-de doh ee-mas-ka*
How do you pronounce ___ that?	それはどう発音しますか。 *soray-wa doh hatsuon shimas-ka*

May I introduce myself? ___	自己紹介してもよろしいですか。 *jiko shohkigh shtay-mo yoroshee des-ka*
My name's... _____	私は…です。 *watashi-wa... des*
What's your name?_____	お名前は？ *onama-e-wa*
May I introduce...? _____	ちょっとご紹介します。…さんです。 *chotto go-shohkigh shimas, ... san des*
This is my wife_____	これは妻です。 *kore-wa tsuma des*
This is my daughter _____	これは娘です。 *kore-wa musumay des*
This is my mother_____	これは母です。 *kore-wa haha des*
This is my friend _____	これは友達です。 *kore-wa tomodachi des*
This is my husband _____	これは夫です。 *kore-wa otto des*
This is my son _____	これは息子です。 *kore-wa musko des*
This is my father _____	これは父です。 *kore-wa chichi des*
How do you do _____	初めまして。どうぞよろしく。 *hajime-mashtay, dohzo yoroshku*
Pleased to meet you_____	お目にかかれて嬉しいです。 *omay-ni kakaretay ureshee des*
Where are you from? _____	お国はどちらですか。 *okuni-wa dochira des-ka*
I'm from the U.S.A. _____	アメリカです。 *Amerika desu*
What city do you live in? _	どこにお住まいですか。 *doko-ni osu-migh des-ka*
In..._____	…に *... ni*
It's near... _____	それは…に近い所です。 *soray-wa ... ni chi-kigh tokoro des*
Have you been here _____ long?	もうお長いのですか。 *moh onagai no des-ka*
A few days _____	二三日です。 *ni san nichi des*
How long are you _____ staying here?	どのぐらいここにおられますか。 *dono gurigh koko-ni oraremas-ka*
We're leaving tomorrow __	明日立ちます。 *ashta tachimas*
We're probably leaving __ in two weeks	二週間後に立つつもりです。 *nishookan-go ni tatsu tsumori des*
Where are you staying?____	どこにお泊りですか。 *doko-ni otomari des-ka*
In a hotel _____	ホテルに *hoteru-ni*
With friends _____	友達の所に *tomodachi-no tokoro-ni*
With relatives _____	親戚の所に *shinseki-no tokoro-ni*

Conversation

Are you here on your own?	一人で来られましたか。 *shtori-day koraremashta-ka*
Are you here with your family?	ご家族とここに来ましたか。 *gokazoku-to koko-ni kimashta-ka*
I'm on my own	一人です。 *shtori des*
I'm with my wife	妻と来ました。 *tsuma-to kimashta*
I'm with my husband	夫と来ました。 *otto-to kimashta*
I'm with my family	家族と来ました。 *kazoku-to kimashta*
I'm with a friend/friends	友達と来ました。 *tomodachi-to kimashta*
Are you married?	結婚していますか。 *kekkon shtay imas-ka*
Do you have a steady boyfriend/girlfriend?	恋人いるの *koi-bito iru-no*
(female) That's none of your business	関係ないでしょ！ *(f) kankay-na-i desho*
(male) That's none of your business	関係ないだろ！ *(m) kankay-na-i daroh*
I'm married	結婚しています。 *kekkon shtay imasu*
– single	一人者です。 *shtorimono des*
– separated/divorced	離婚しています。 *rikon shtay imas*
– a widow/widower	未亡人／やもめです。 *miboh-jin/yamomay des*
I live with someone	恋人と住んでいます。 *koibito-to sunday imas*
Do you have any children?	お子さんは？ *oko-san-wa*
Do you have any grandchildren?	お孫さんは？ *omago-san-wa*
How old are you?	失礼ですが、何歳ですか。 *shitsuray des-nga, nansigh des-ka*
How old is she?	女の子はいくつですか。 *onna-no-ko wa ikutsu des-ka*
How old is he?	男の子はいくつですか。 *otoko-no-ko wa ikutsu des-ka*
I'm...	…歳です。 *...sigh des*
She's/he's...	…歳です。 *...sigh des*
What do you do for a living?	お仕事は何ですか。 *oshigoto-wa nan des-ka*
I work in an office	会社で働いています。 *kighsha-de hata-right-tay imas*
I'm a student/ I'm at school	学生です。 *gaksay des*
I'm unemployed	無職です。 *mushoku des*
I'm retired	退職しました。 *tigh-shoku shimashta*

I'm on a disability pension	障害者です。
	shoh-gigh-sha des
I'm a housewife	主婦です。
	shufu des
Do you like your job?	お仕事は面白いですか。
	o-shigoto-wa omoshiroi des-ka
Most of the time	たいがいは。
	tigh-gigh-wa
I usually do, but I prefer vacations	まあまあですが、休みの方が面白いですよね。
	mah mah des-nga, yasumi-no hoh-nga
	omoshiroi des-yo-ne

3 .3 Starting/ending a conversation

Excuse me	すみませんが
	sumimasen-nga
Excuse me, could you help me?	すみませんが、助けて下さい。
	sumimasen-nga, tasketay kuda-sigh
Yes, what's the problem?	どうしましたか。
	doh shimashta-ka
What can I do for you?	何かご用でしょうか。
	nani-ka goyoh deshoh-ka
Sorry, I don't have time now	急ぎますので、すみません。
	isogimas noday, sumimasen
Do you have a light?	火をおもちですか。
	hi-o mochi des-ka
May I join you?	ご一緒させていただいてもよろしいですか。
	goissho sasete itadigh-tay-mo yoroshee des-ka
Could you take a picture of me/us?	写真をとってくださいますか。
	shashin-o tottay kudasaimas-ka
Press this button	このボタンを押して下さい。
	kono botan-o oshtay kuda-sigh
(female) Leave me alone	ほっといてよ！
	hotto itay-yo
(male) Leave me alone	ほっといてくれよ！
	hotto itay kuray-yo
(female) Get lost	あっちいってよ！
	achi ittay-yo
(male) Get lost	あっちいけよ！
	achi ikay-yo
(female) Go away or I'll scream	行かないと叫ぶわよ！
	ikanai-to, sakebu-wa-yo
(male) Go away or I'll yell	行かないと叫ぶよ！
	ikanai-to, sakebu-yo

3 .4 Congratulations and condolences

Happy birthday/many happy returns	お誕生日おめでとうございます。
	otanjohbi omedetoh gozaimas
Please accept my condolences	心からお悔やみ申し上げます。
	kokoro-kara o-kuyami mohshi-agemas

3 .5 A chat about the weather

See also 1.5 The weather

It's so hot today! _____	今日は暑いですね。
	kyoh-wa atsui des-ne
It's so cold toady! _____	今日は寒いですね。
	kyoh-wa samui des-ne
Nice weather, isn't it?_____	いい天気ですね。
	ee tenki des-ne
What a wind! _____	すごい風ですね。
	sugoi kazay des-ne
All that rain! _____	すごい雨ですね。
	sugoi amay des-ne
All that snow!_____	雪が凄いですね。
	yuki-wa sugoi des-ne
All that fog! _____	深い霧ですね。
	fukigh kiri des-ne
Has the weather been _____ like this for long here?	この天気はもう長いんですか。
	kono tenki-wa moh nagai-n des-ka
Is it always this hot _____ here?	この辺はいつも暑いんですか。
	kono hen-wa itsumo atsui-n des-ka
Is it always this cold _____ here?	この辺はいつも寒いんですか。
	kono hen-wa itsumo samui-n des-ka
Is it always this dry here? __	この辺はいつも雨が少ないんですか。
	kono hen-wa itsumo amay-nga sukunai-n des-ka
Is it always this wet here?__	この辺はいつも雨が多いですか。
	kono hen-wa itsumo amay-nga oh-ee des-ka

3 .6 Hobbies

Do you have any _____ hobbies?	趣味は？
	shoomi-wa
I like knitting _____	編みものが好きです。
	amimono-ga ski des
I like reading_____	読書が好きです。
	dokusho-ga ski des
I like photography _____	写真をとるのが好きです。
	shashin-o toru-no-ga ski de
I like music _____	音楽が好きです。
	ongaku-ga ski des
I like playing the guitar ____	ギターを弾くのが好きです。
	gitah-o hiku-no-ga ski des
I like playing the piano ____	ピアノを弾くのが好きです。
	piano-o hiku-no-ga ski des
I like going to the _____ movies	映画を見に行くのが好きです。
	ayga-o mi-ni iku-no-ga ski des
I like travelling _____	旅行するのが好きです。
	ryokoh suru-no-ga ski des
I like playing sports_____	スポーツが好きです。
	spohtsu-ga ski des
I like fishing_____	つりに行くのが好きです。
	tsuri-ni iku-no-ga ski des
I like walking_____	散歩するのが好きです。
	sampo suru-no-ga ski des

.7 Being the host(ess)

See also 4 Eating out

Can I offer you a drink? ___	何かお飲みになりませんか。 *nani-ka onomi-ni-narimasen-ka*
What would you like to ___ drink?	何をお飲みになりますか。 *nani-o onomi-ni narimas-ka*
Would you like a _____ cigarette?	タバコはいかがですか。 *tabako-wa ikaga des-ka*
Would you like a cigar? ___	葉巻はいかがですか。 *hamaki-wa ikaga des-ka*
Something non-alcoholic, ___ please	アルコールなしの飲み物を下さい。 *arukohru-nashi no nomimono-o kuda-sigh*
I don't smoke _____	たばこは吸いません。 *tabako-wa suimasen*

.8 Invitations

Are you doing anything ___ tonight?	もう今晩の予定は何か決めたの。 *moh komban-no yotay-wa nani-ka kimeta-no*
Do you have any plans ___ for today/this afternoon?	もう今日の計画は出来ましたか。 *moh kyoh-no kaykaku-wa dekimashta-ka*
Do you have any plans ___ for tonight?	もう今晩の計画は出来ましたか。 *moh komban-no kaykaku-wa dekimashta-ka*
Would you like to go _____ out with me?	一緒に出かけませんか。 *isshoh-ni dekakemasen-ka*
Would you like to go _____ dancing with me?	一緒にダンスに行きませんか。 *isshoh-ni dansu-ni ikimasen-ka*
Would you like to have ___ lunch/dinner with me?	一緒に食べませんか。 *isshoh-ni tabemasen-ka*
Would you like to come ___ to the beach with me?	一緒に海岸に行きませんか。 *isshoh-ni kighgan-ni ikimasen-ka*
Would you like to come ___ into town with us?	一緒に町へ行きませんか。 *isshoh-ni machi-e ikimasen-ka*
Would you like to come ___ and see some friends with us?	一緒に友達の所に行きませんか。 *isshoh-ni tomodachi-no tokoro-ni ikimasen-ka*
I don't dance_____	踊りません。 *odorimasen*
Shall we sit at the bar? ___	バーに座らない？ *bah-ni suwara-nigh?*
Shall we get something ___ to drink?	何か飲みましょうか。 *nani-ka nomi-mashoh-ka*
Shall we go for a walk? ___	散歩に行きましょうか。 *sampoh-ni iki-mashoh-ka*
Shall we go for a drive? ___	ドライブに行きましょうか。 *drighb-ni iki-mashoh-ka*
Yes, all right _____	いいね。 *ee-ne*
Good idea _____	いい考え *ee kangae*
No (thank you) _____	いいえ、けっこうです *ee-ye, kekkoh des*
Maybe later_____	多分今度。 *tabun kondo*

3 Conversation

(female) I don't feel like it	興味がないわ。
	kyohmi-nga nigh-wa
(male) I don't feel like it	興味がないよ。
	kyohmi-nga nigh-yo
(female) I don't have time	時間がないわ。
	jikan-nga nigh-wa
(male) I don't have time	時間がないよ。
	jikan-nga nigh-yo
I already have a date	もう他の約束が。
	moh hoka-no yakusoku-nga
I'm not very good at dancing	ダンスは下手です。
	dans-wa heta-des
I'm not very good at volleyball	バレーボールは下手です。
	baray-bohru-wa heta-des
I can't swim	泳げません。
	oyogemasen

3.9 Paying a compliment

You look wonderful!	おきれいですね。
	okiray des-ne
I like your car!	いい車ですね！
	ee kuruma des-ne
What a sweet child!	何てかわいい赤ちゃんでしょう。
	nantay kawa-ee akachan deshoh
You're a wonderful dancer!	ダンスが上手ですね。
	dans-ga johzu des-ne
You're a wonderful cook!	料理が上手ですね。
	ryohri-ga johzu des-ne
You're a terrific tennis player!	テニスが上手ですね。
	tenisu-ga johzu des-ne

3.10 Intimate comments/questions

I like being with you	一緒にいるのが楽しい。
	isshoh-ni iru-no-ga tanoshee
(female) I've missed you so much	とっても寂しかったわ。
	tottemo sabishikatta-wa
(male) I've missed you so much	とっても寂しかったよ。
	tottemo sabishikatta-yo
(female) I dreamt about you	あなたを夢にみたわ。
	anata-o yumay-ni mita-wa
(male) I dreamt about you	君を夢にみたよ。
	kimi-o yumay-ni mita-yo
You're pretty!	きれいだよ。
	kiray da-yo
(female) You're nice	すてきよ。
	steki-yo
(male) You're nice	すてきだよ。
	steki da-yo
You're sexy	セクシー。
	sekshee
(female) Look at me	私を見て。
	watashi-o mitay
(male) Look at me	僕を見て。
	boku-o mitay

You have such beautiful __ eyes	きれいな瞳だね。
	kiray-na shtomi da-ne
(female) I'm crazy about __ you	あなたに夢中なの。
	anata-ni muchoo na no
(male) I'm crazy about __ you	君に夢中なんだ。
	kimi-ni muchoo nanda
I love you_____	愛してる。
	igh-shteru
(female) I love you too_____	私も。
	watashi-mo
(male) I love you too _____	僕も。
	boku-mo
(female) I don't feel as __ strongly about you	私の気持ちは違うの。
	watashi-no kimochi-wa chigau-no
(male) I don't feel as _____ strongly about you	僕の気持ちは違うんだ。
	boku-no kimochi-wa chigaun-da
I already have a _____ boyfriend/girlfriend	もう恋人がいます。
	moh koibito-ga imas
I'm not ready for that_____	もう少し待って。
	moh skoshi mattay
(female) This is going _____ too fast for me	すごく早過ぎるの。
	sugoku haya-suguru-no
(male) This is going _____ too fast for me	すごく早過ぎるよ。
	sugoku haya-suguru-yo
(female) Take your hands __ off me	触らないで。
	sawara-nigh-day
Okay, no problem _____	いいよ。
	ee-yo
Will you stay with me _____ tonight?	今夜一緒に泊まらない？
	konya issoh-ni tomara-nigh?
I'd like to go to bed _____ with you	愛したい。
	igh-shtigh
Only if we use a condom __	コンドームを使ってくれるなら。
	kondom-o tsukattay kureru-nara
We have to be careful _____ about AIDS	エイズのこともあるからね。
	ayzu-no koto-mo aru kara-ne
(female) That's what they __ all say	男って皆そういうのね。
	otokot-tay mina soh yoo no-ne
(female) We shouldn't _____ take any risks	危険は避けましょうよ。
	kiken-wa sakay mashoh-yo
(male) We shouldn't _____ take any risks	危険は避けようよ。
	kiken-wa sakay-yoh-yo
Do you have a condom? ___	コンドームもってる？
	kondom motteru?
(female) No? In that case __ we won't do it	それなら、やめましょう。
	sore-nara, yamemashoh
(male) No? In that case _____ we won't do it	それなら、やめよう。
	sore-nara, yameyoh

3

Conversation

3 .11 Arrangements

When will I see you again?	またいつ会える。 *mata itsu aeru*
Are you free over the weekend?	この週末おひまですか。 *kono shoomatsu ohima des-ka*
What shall we do?	何か計画しましょうか。 *nani-ka kay-kaku shimashoh-ka*
Where shall we meet?	どこで会いましょうか。 *doko-de aimashoh-ka*
Will you pick me/us up?	車で拾ってくださいますか。 *kuruma-de hirottay kudasaimas-ka*
Shall I pick you up?	車で拾って上げましょうか。 *kuruma-de hirottay agemashoh-ka*
I have to be home by...	…時までに帰らなければなりません。 *...ji-made-ni kaera-nakeraba-narimasen*
(female) I don't want to see you anymore	もう会いたくないわ。 *moh aitaku-nigh-wa*
(male) I don't want to see you anymore	もう会いたくないよ。 *moh aitaku-nigh-yo*

3 .12 Saying good-bye

Can I take you home?	送っていってもいいですか。 *okuttay ittay-mo ee des-ka*
Can I write?	手紙を書いてもいいですか。 *tegami-o kaitay-mo ee des-ka*
Can I call you?	電話をかけてもいいですか。 *denwa-o kaketay-mo ee des-ka*
Will you write to me?	手紙をくれますか。 *tegami-o kuremas-ka*
Will you call me?	電話をくれますか。 *denwa-o kuremas-ka*
Can I have your address?	あなたの住所を教えてくれますか。 *anata-no joosho-o oshietay kuremas-ka*
Can I have your phone number?	あなたの電話番号を教えてくれますか。 *anata-no denwa bango-o oshietay kuremas-ka*
Thanks for everything	いろいろありがとうございました。 *iro-iro arigatoh goza-i-mashta*
It was very nice	とても楽しかったです。 *totemo tanoshikatta des*
Say hello to...	…さんによろしく。 *... san ni yoroshku*
All the best	元気でね。 *genki de-ne*
When will you be back?	いつ帰る？ *itsu kaeru?*
(female) I'll be waiting for you	待ってるわ。 *matteru-wa*
(male) I'll be waiting for you	待ってるよ。 *matteru-yo*
(female) I'd like to see you again	また会いたいわ。 *mata ai-tigh-wa*

(male) I'd like to see _____ you again	また会いたいなあ。
	mata ai-tigh-nah
This is our address. If _____ you're ever in the U.S., you'd be more than welcome	私たちの住所です。いつでもイギリスにいらしたらどうぞ。
	watashi-tachi-no joosho des. itsu-demo igirisu-ni irashtara dohzo

Conversation

Eating out

Eating out

● **Large cities like Tokyo** offer a vast selection of restaurants with food from all over the world. American fast food chain outlets can be found in most neighborhoods near railway stations. Very popular too are "family restaurants", where wide-ranging menus offer budget-priced dishes to suit the whole family. All department stores have two or more restaurant floors, with individual restaurants serving most varieties of Japanese, Chinese, and Western food. In addition there is usually a large customers' restaurant, again with a wide selection. Food selection is made very easy in Japan because all restaurants display in their window wax models of the dishes offered and their prices. Family restaurants provide a fully-illustrated menu. Only very expensive, upscale restaurants do not do this. Children are almost always welcome at local restaurants and those in the popular shopping centers and stations. Traditional restaurants with *tatami* (straw-matted) floors are a benefit for those with babies.

4 **.1 O**n arrival

I'd like to reserve a table for seven o'clock, please	七時にテーブルを予約したいのですが。 *shichiji-ni tehburu-o yoyaku shi-tigh no des-nga*
I'd like a table for two, please	二人用のテーブルをお願いします。 *futari-yoh-no tehburu-o onegigh shimas*
We've reserved _____	予約しました。 *yoyaku shimashta*
We haven't reserved _____	予約していません。 *yoyaku shtay imasen*
What time does the _____ restaurant open	レストランは何時からオープンですか。 *restoran-wa nanji-kara ohpen des-ka*
What time does the _____ restaurant close?	レストランは何時までですか。 *restoran-wa nanji maday des-ka*
Can we wait for a table? ___	テーブルが空くまで待ちたいのですが。 *tehburu-ga aku-made machi-tigh no des-nga*
Do we have to wait long? __	長く待ちますか。 *nagaku machimas-ka*
Is this seat taken? _____	この席、空いてますか。 *kono seki ightay imas-ka*
Could we sit here? _____	ここに座ってもいいですか。 *koko-ni suwatte-mo ee des-ka*
Could we sit there?_____	あそこに座ってもいいですか。 *asoko-ni suwatte-mo ee des-ka*
Can we sit by the _____ window?	窓ぎわに座ってもいいですか。 *mado-giwa-ni suwatte-mo ee des-ka*

ご予約ですか_____	Do you have a reservation?
お名前は_____	What name, please?
こちらへ_____	This way, please
このテーブルは予約済みです。_____	This table is reserved
15分お待ちいただくと_____ テーブルが空きます。	We'll have a table free in fifteen minutes.
（バーで）_____ お待ちになりますか	Would you like to wait (at the bar)?

Can we eat outside? _____ 外でも食べられますか。
soto demo taberaremas-ka

Do you have another _____ 椅子もう一個ありますか。
chair for us? *isu moh ikko arimas-ka*

Do you have a highchair? __ 子供用の椅子がありますか。
kodomo-yoh-no isu-ga arimas-ka

Could you warm up this ___ すみませんが、このびんを暖めてくれますか。
bottle/jar for me? *sumimasen-ga, kono bin-o atatametay kure-mas-ka*

Not too hot, please _____ 熱過ぎないように。
atsu-suginigh yoh-ni

Is there somewhere I _____ ベビールームありますか。
can change the baby's *bebee-room arimas-ka*
diaper?

Where are the restrooms? _ トイレはどこですか。
toireh-wa doko des-ka

4 .2 Ordering

Waiter! _____ ウェーターさん
wehtah-san!

Waitress! _____ ウェートレスさん
wehtres-san!

We'd like something _____ 何か食べたいんですが。
to eat *nani-ka tabe-tigh-n des-nga*

We'd like a drink _____ 何か飲みたいんですが。
nani-ka nomi-tigh-n des-nga

Could I have a quick _____ 何か速く出来る品はありますか。
meal? *nani-ka hayaku dekiru shina-wa arimas-ka*

We don't have much _____ 急いでいるのですが。
time *isoiday iru no des-nga*

We'd like to have a _____ 先ず何か飲みたいんですが
drink first *mazu nani-ka nomi-tig-n des-nga*

Do you have a menu _____ 英語のメニューはありますか。
in English? *aygo no menyoo-wa arimas-ka*

Do you have a dish _____ 今日のメニューはありますか。
of the day? *kyoh no menyoo-wa arimas-ka*

We haven't made a _____ まだ決りません。
choice yet *mada kimarimasen*

What do you _____ お薦め品は何ですか。
recommend? *o-susume-hin-wa nan des-ka*

What are the specials? _____ 特別料理は何ですか。
tokubetsu ryohri-wa nan des-ka

I don't like... _____ …は好きじゃないんです。
... wa ski ja nigh-n des

I don't like fish _____ 魚は好きじゃないんです。
sakana-wa ski ja nigh-n des

I don't like meat_____ 肉は好きじゃないんです。
niku-wa ski ja nigh-n des

What's this? _____ これは何ですか。
koray-wa nan des-ka

Does it have...in it? _____ …が入っていますか。
... nga ha-ittay imas-ka

Is this a hot dish? _____ この料理は暖かいですか。
kono ryohri-wa atata-kigh des-ka

Is this a cold dish? _____ この料理は冷たいですか。
kono ryohri-wa tsume-tigh des-ka

Is this sweet? _____ この料理は甘いですか。
kono ryohri-wa a-migh des-ka

Is this spicy? _____ この料理はからいですか。
kono ryohri-wa ka-righ des-ka

Do you have anything _____ 他に何かありますか。
else, please? *hoka-ni nani-ka arimas-ka*

I'm on a salt-free diet _____ 塩ぬきでお願いします。
sheeo-nuki-de onegai-shimas

I can't eat pork _____ 豚肉は食べられません。
butaniku-wa taberare-masen

– sugar _____ 砂糖は食べられません。
satoh-wa taberare-masen

– fatty foods _____ 油っぽい料理は食べられません。
aburap-poy ryohri-wa taberare-masen

– (hot) spices _____ (辛い) スパイスは食べられません。
(karigh) spighs-wa taberare-masen

I'll/we'll have what those __ あの人と同じ料理を、お願いします。
people are having *ano-shto-to onaji ryohri-o onegai-shimas*

I'd like... _____ …お願いします。
... onegai-shimas

Do you have a knife _____ ナイフとフォークありますか。
and fork? *nighf to fohk arimas-ka*

A little more rice please____ ご飯もう少しお願いします。
gohan moh skoshi onegai-shimas

Another glass of water, ___ 水もう一杯お願いします。
please *mizu moh ip-pigh onegai-shimas*

One more please_____ もう一つお願いします。
moh hitotsu onegai-shimas

Do you have salt and _____ 塩と胡椒ありますか。
pepper? *sheeo to koshoh arimas-ka*

Do you have a napkin? ____ ナプキンありますか。
napukin arimas-ka

Do you have a spoon?_____ スプーンありますか。
spoon arimas-ka

Do you have an ashtray? __ 灰皿ありますか。
high-zara arimas-ka

Do you have any _____ マッチありますか。
matches? *match arimas-ka*

Do you have any _____ つまようじありますか。
toothpicks? *tsuma-yohji arimas-ka*

Can I have a glass of _____ 水一杯お願いします。
water, please *mizu ippigh onegai-shimas*

Do you have a straw? _____ ストローありますか。
stroh arimas-ka

Let's begin_____ いただきましょう。
itadakimashoh

Cheers!_____ 乾杯
kam-pigh

The next round's on me ___ 今度は私がおごります。
kondo-wa watashi-nga ogorimas

4.3 The bill

See also 8.2 Settling the bill

How much is this dish?	この料理はいくらですか。 *kono ryohri-wa ikura des-ka*
Could I have the bill, please?	お勘定、お願いします。 *okanjoh onegigh-shimas*
All together	全部で *zembu-de*
Everyone pays separately	各自が払いますので。 *kakuji-nga haraimas no-de*
Could we have the menu again, please?	もう一回メニューを見せて下さい。 *moh ik-kigh menyoo-o misetay kuda-sigh*
The...is not on the bill	…が入っていません。 *... ga hight-tay imasen*

4.4 Complaints

It's taking a very long time	ずいぶん長くかかっていますね。 *zuibun nagaku kakattay imas-ne*
We've been here an hour already	もう一時間も待っています。 *moh ichi-jikan-mo mattay imas*
This must be a mistake	これは間違いでしょう。 *koray-wa machigigh deshoh*
This is not what I ordered	これは注文しませんでした。 *koray-wa choomon shimasen deshta*
I ordered...	…を注文しました。 *... o choomon shimashta*
There's a dish missing	料理が一品不足です。 *ryohri-ga ippin fusoku des*
This is broken	これは壊れています。 *kore-wa kowarete-imas*
This is not clean	ちょっとこれきたないのですが。 *chotto koray kita-nigh no des-nga*
The food's cold	料理が冷たいんです。 *ryohri-ga tsume-tigh-n des*
– not fresh	これは新鮮じゃないです。 *koray-wa shinsen ja nigh des*
– too salty	これは塩辛いです。 *koray-wa sheeo ka-righ des*
– too sweet	これは甘過ぎます。 *koray-wa ama-sugimas*
– too spicy	これは辛過ぎます。 *koray-wa kara-sugimas*
The meat's not done	肉は焼き足りません。 *niku-wa yaki-tarimasen*
– overdone	肉は焼き過ぎです。 *niku-wa yaki-sugi des*
– tough	肉が堅いんです。 *niku-ga ka-tigh-n des*
– spoiled	肉がくさっています。 *niku-ga kusattay imas*
Could I have something else instead of this?	代わりの品を下さいませんか。 *kawari-no shina-o kudasaimasen-ka*
The bill/this amount is not right	勘定が合いません。 *kanjoh-nga aimasen*

We didn't have this _____	これは食べませんでした。
	koray-wa tabe-masen deshta
There's no paper in _____ the restroom	トイレットペーパーがないんです。
	toiretto-pehpah-ga nigh-n des
Will you get the _____ manager, please?	責任者を呼んでください。
	sekinin-sha-o yonday kuda-sigh

4 .5 Paying a compliment

That was a wonderful _____ meal	とてもおいしかったです。
	totemo oishikatta-des
The food was excellent ____	ごちそうさまでした。
	gochisoh sama deshta
The...in particular was ____ delicious	特に…がとてもおいしかったです。
	toku-ni ... nga totemo oishikatta-des

4 .6 The menu

The following are some of the most popular Japanese dishes.

しゃぶしゃぶ   Shabu shabu
Thin strips of pork or lamb and various vegetables cooked in front of you in boiling water and eaten in dipping sauces.

焼き鳥   Yakitori
Marinated chicken pieces on skewers, cooked over a brazier.

味噌汁   Misoshiru
Soup made from miso (paste of fermented soy beans) with tofu and vegetables such as cabbage and small mushrooms.

うどん、そば   Udon, soba
Thick white and thin brown noodles respectively. Served either cold with dipping sauces (good in summer) or warm in a soup.

茶わんむし   Chawan-mushi
Fish and vegetables steamed in an egg custard.

豚カツ   Tonkatsu
Pork cutlets fried in breadcrumbs and served with a thick brown sauce.

親子どんぶり   Oyako donburi
Chicken and egg served on rice. A popular lunch dish.

カレーライス   Karee raisu (karay righ-su)
The Japanese version of curry and rice. Usually beef, chicken, or pork pieces in a curry sauce.

5

On the road

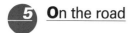

.1 **A**sking for directions

Excuse me, could I ask you something?	すみませんが *sumimasen-nga*
I've lost my way	道に迷ってしまったんですが。 *michi-ni mayottay shimattan-des-nga*
Is there a(n)... around here?	この辺に…がありますか。 *kono hen-ni ... ga arimas-ka*
Is this the way to...?	この道は…へ行きますか。 *kono michi-wa ... e ikimas-ka*
Could you tell me how to get to the... (name of place)by car/on foot?	…へどう行くか教えて下さいませんか。 *... e doh iku-ka oshietay kudasai-masen-ka*
What's the quickest way to...?	…への一番速い道はどう行きますか。 *... e no ichiban hayai michi-wa doh ikimas-ka*
How many kilometers is it to...?	…まで何キロぐらいですか。 *... maday nankiro-gurigh-n des-ka*
Could you point it out on the map?	この地図で指差して下さい。 *kono chizu-de yubi-sashtay kuda-sigh*
My children are entered on this passport	子供はこのパスポートに記入してあります。 *kodomo-wa kono pas-pohto-ni kinyoo shitay arimas*
I'm travelling through	通過していきます。 *tsooka shtay imas*

すみませんが、知りません。	I don't know, I don't know my way around here
道が違います。	You're going the wrong way
…に戻らなければなりません。	You have to go back to...
そこに着いたら、もう一度尋ねてください。	When you get there, ask again

真っ直ぐ straight ahead	信号 the traffic light	高架橋 the overpass
左に left	トンネル the tunnel	橋 the bridge
右に right	一旦停止標識 the 'yield' sign	踏切 the grade crossing/ the barrier gates
渡って cross	建物／ビル the building	矢印 the arrow
交差点 the intersection	曲がり角で at the corner	
道 the street	川 the river	

5.2 Customs

A passport is necessary for all visitors to Japan. Citizens of most European countries do not need a visa if they are staying as tourists up to 90 days. Visitors from the US, Canada, and New Zealand need a visa for visits of over 90 days. They are easily obtainable and free. Visitors from Australia need a visa for any visit. Drugs, firearms, and pornography may not be taken into Japan. Non-residents can take in duty-free 400 cigarettes, or 100 cigars, or 500g of tobacco; 3 bottles of alcohol (760cc each); 50g perfume; and other goods up to 200,000 yen in value. Personal possessions are exempt.

パスポートを見せて下さい。＿＿＿＿＿＿	Your passport, please
ビザを見せて下さい。＿＿＿＿＿＿＿＿	Your visa, please
どこへ行きますか。＿＿＿＿＿＿＿＿＿	Where are you heading?
どのくらい滞在しますか。＿＿＿＿＿＿	How long are you planning to stay?
申告する品はありますか。＿＿＿＿＿＿	Do you have anything to declare?
これを開けて見せて下さい。＿＿＿＿＿	Open this, please

I'm going on vacation to... ＿	休暇で…へ行きます。
	kyooka-de ... e ikimas
I'm on a business trip ＿＿＿	出張です。
	shutchoh des
I don't know how long ＿＿＿ I'll be staying yet	どのぐらい長くいるかまだ分かりません。
	dono-gurigh nagaku iru-ka mada wakarimasen
I'll be staying here ＿＿＿＿ for a weekend	この週末だけいます。
	kono shoo-mats dakay imas
– for a few days ＿＿＿＿＿	二、三日います。
	ni, san-nichi imas
– for a week＿＿＿＿＿＿＿	一週間います。
	i-shookan imas
– for two weeks ＿＿＿＿＿	二週間います。
	ni-shookan imas
I've got nothing ＿＿＿＿＿ to declare	何も申告する物はありません。
	nani-mo shinkoku suru mono-wa arimasen
I've got...with me＿＿＿＿＿	…を持っています。
	... o mottay imas
– ...100 cigarettes＿＿＿＿＿	たばこは百本あります。
	tabako-wa hyappon arimas
– ...1 bottle of... ＿＿＿＿＿	…は一本あります。
	... wa ippon arimas
– some souvenirs ＿＿＿＿＿	二、三のおみやげがあります。
	ni, san-no omiyagay-nga arimas
These are personal ＿＿＿＿ possessions	これは自分で使う物です。
	koray-wa jibun-de tsukau mono des
These are not new ＿＿＿＿	これは新しくありません。
	koray-wa ata-rashiku arimasen
Here's the receipt ＿＿＿＿＿	領収書です。
	ryohshoo-sho des

How much import tax _____ do I have to pay?	輸入税はいくらですか。
	yunyoo-zay-wa ikura des-ka
	行ってもいいですか。
Can I go now? _____	*ittay-mo ee des-ka*

.3 Luggage

Porter! _____	ポーターさん！
	pohtah-san
Could you take this _____ luggage to...?	この荷物を…に持って行って下さい。
	kono nimots-o ... ni mottay ittay kuda-sigh
How much do I _____ owe you?	いくらですか。
	ikura des-ka
Where can I find a _____ luggage cart?	台車はどこにありますか。
	dighsha-wa doko-ni arimas-ka
Could you store this _____ luggage for me?	この荷物を預かってもらえますか。
	kono nimots-o azukattay mo-rae-mas-ka
Where are the luggage _____ lockers?	ロッカーはどこですか。
	rokkah-wa doko des-ka
I can't get the locker _____ open	ロッカーが空きません。
	rokkah-ga akimasen
How much is it per _____ item per day?	一日一個いくらですか。
	ichinichi ikko ikura des-ka
This is not my _____ bag/suitcase	私のカバンではありません。
	watashi-no kaban de wa arimasen
There's one bag/ _____ suitcase missing still	カバンが一つ足りません。
	kaban-ga hitots tarimasen
My suitcase is damaged _____	カバンが壊れています。
	kaban-ga kowarete-imasu

.4 The car

See the diagram on page 45.

An international driving license is required to drive in Japan. Traffic drives on the left. The speed limit varies but is usually around 40 kph in urban areas and 80 kph on highways; it is 100 kph on highways. Driving can be complicated because, on some of the highways, signs are written in Japanese characters. Highways are expensive, and there are many toll roads, especially in scenic areas.

On the road

The parts of a car
(the diagram shows the numbered parts)

1 battery	バッテリー	*batteree*
2 rear light	バック・ライト	*bakku-right*
3 rear-view mirror	バック・ミラー	*bakku-mirah*
backup light	バックアップ・ライト	*bakku-upp-right*
4 antenna	アンテナ	*antena*
car radio	ラジオ	*rajio*
5 gas tank	燃料タンク／ガソリン・タンク	*nenryoh- tanku/gasorin-tanku*
6 spark plugs	スパーク・プラグ	*spahk puragu*
fuel filter/pump	燃料フィルター／ポンプ	*nenryoh firutah/pomp*
7 side mirror	サイド・ミラー	*sighdo-mirah*
8 bumper	バンパー	*banpah*
carburetor	キャブレター	*kyaburetah*
crankcase	クランク・ケース	*krank-kays*
cylinder	シリンダー	*shirindah*
ignition	イグニッション	*igunishon*
warning light	警告灯	*kay-koku-toh*
generator	発電器	*hats-den-ki*
accelerator	アクセル	*akuseru*
handbrake	ハンドブレーキ	*hando-burayki*
valve	弁／バルブ	*ben/barubu*
9 silencer	マフラー／消音器	*mufurah/shoh-on-ki*
10 trunk	トランク	*toranku*
11 headlight	ヘッド・ライト	*heddo-right*
crank shaft	クランクシャフト	*kurank-shafuto*
12 air filter	エア・フィルター	*e-a firutah*
fog lamp	フォグ・ランプ	*fog-rampu*
13 engine block	エンジン	*enjin*
camshaft	カムシャフト	*kamu-shafuto*
oil filter/pump	オイル・フィルター／ポンプ	*oyru-firutah/pomp*
dipstick	オイルゲージ	*oyru-gayji*
pedal	ペダル	*pedaru*
14 door	ドア	*do-a*
15 radiator	ラジエーター	*raji-aytah*
16 brake disc	ブレーキ・ディスク	*burayk-disk*
spare wheel	スペア・タイヤ	*supe-a tigh-a*
17 indicator	方向指示器	*hohkoh-shijiki*
18 windshield wiper	ワイパー	*wigh-pah*
19 shock absorbers	ショック・アブソーバー	*shokk-absohbah*
sunroof	サンルーフ	*sanroof*
spoiler	スポイラー	*spoy-rah*
starter motor	スターターモーター	*stahtah-mohtah*
20 steering column	ステアリング・コラム	*stearing-koram*
21 exhaust pipe	排気管	*high-ki-kan*
22 seat belt	シートベルト	*sheet-beruto*
fan	ファン	*fan*
23 distributor cables	ディストリビューター・ケーブル	*distribyutah kayburu*
24 gear shift	シフト・レバー	*shift-rebah*

44

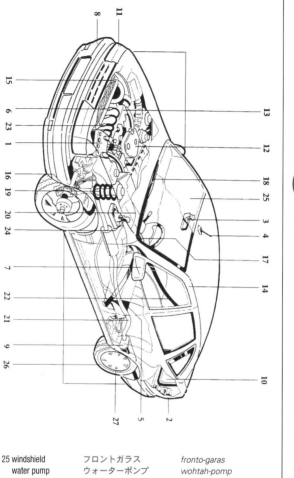

25	windshield	フロントガラス	*fronto-garas*
	water pump	ウォーターポンプ	*wohtah-pomp*
26	wheel	タイヤ	*tigh-yah*
27	hubcap	ハブ・キャップ	*hab-kyapp*
	piston	ピストン	*piston*

How many kilometers _____ to the next gas station, please?	次のガソリン・スタンドまで何キロぐらいですか。 *tsugi-no gasorin-sutando-maday nankiro gurigh des-ka*
I would like...liters of..., _____ please	…を…リットルお願いします。 *... o ...rittoru onegigh-shimas*
– super _____	ハイオク *high-oku*
– leaded _____	有鉛 *yoo-en*
– unleaded _____	無鉛 *mu-en*
– diesel _____	ディーゼル *dee-zeru*
I would like...yen's _____ worth of gas, please	…円だけガソリンお願いします。 *...en dakay gasorin o-negigh-shimas*
Fill her up, please _____	満タンお願いします。 *mantan o-negigh-shimas*
Could you check...? _____	…を点検して下さい。 *... o tenken shitay kuda-sigh*
– the oil level _____	オイル *oyru*
– the tire pressure _____	タイヤの空気圧 *tighya-no kooki-ats*
Could you change _____ the oil, please?	オイルを替えてくれますか。 *oyru-o ka-etay kuremas-ka*
Could you clean the _____ windows/the windshield, please?	(フロント)ガラスをふいてくれますか。 *(fronto) garas-o fu-itay kuremas-ka*
Could you wash the _____ car, please?	洗車お願いします。 *sensha o-negigh-shimas*

.6 Breakdown and repairs

I'm having car trouble. Could you give me a hand?	車が故障しました。手伝ってくださいませんか。 *kuruma-nga koshoh shimashta. tetsu-dattay kudasa-e-masen-ka*
I've run out of gas _____	ガソリンがないんですが *gasorin-ga nigh-n des-nga*
I've locked the keys _____ in the car	鍵を車の中に忘れてしまいました。 *kagi-o kuruma-no naka-ni wasuretay shima-imashta*
The car/motorcycle/ _____ moped won't start	エンジンがかかりません。 *enjin-nga kakarimasen*
Could you call a garage _____ for me, please?	修理屋を呼んでくれませんか。 *shoori-ya-o yonday kuremasen-ka*
Could you give me _____ a lift to...?	…まで乗せて下さいませんか。 *... maday nosetay kudasa-e-masen-ka*
– a garage? _____	修理屋 *shoori-ya*
– into town? _____	町 *machi*
– a phone booth? _____	電話ボックス *denwa boks*

Can we take my bicycle? ___	自転車も持って行けますか。 *jitensha-mo mottay ikemas-ka*
– scooter ___	スクーターも持って行けますか。 *skootah-mo mottay ikemas-ka*
Could you tow me ___ to a garage?	修理屋まで車を運んで下さいませんか。 *shoori-ya-maday kuruma-o hakonday kudasa-e-masen-ka*
There's probably ___ something wrong with... (See 5.4 and 5.7)	…が悪いんですが。 *... ga warui-n des-nga*
Can you fix it? ___	修理できますか。 *shoori dekimas-ka*
Could you fix my tire? ___	タイヤを修理して下さい。 *tigh-ya-o shoori shtay kuda-sigh*
Could you change this ___ wheel?	このタイヤを交換して下さい。 *kono tigh-ya-o kohkan shtay kuda-sigh*
Can you fix it so it'll ___ get me to...?	…へ行けるまでの修理をお願いできますか。 *... e ikeru maday-no shoori-o onegigh-deki mas-ka*
Which garage can ___ help me?	どの修理屋で修理出来ますか。 *dono shoori-ya-de shoori dekimas-ka*
When will my car/ ___ bicycle be ready?	いつ取りに来れますか。 *its tori-ni koremas-ka*
Can I wait for it here? ___	ここで待てますか。 *koko-de matemas-ka*
How much will it cost? ___	いくらかかりますか。 *ikura kakarimas-ka*
Could you itemize ___ the bill?	勘定を明細に書いて下さい。 *kanjoh-o maysigh-ni kigh-tay kuda-sigh*
Can I have a receipt ___ for the insurance?	保険のための領収書を下さい。 *hoken-no tamay-no ryohshoo-sho-o kuda-sigh*

On the road

5 .7 The bicycle/moped

See the diagram on page 49.

The bicycle is used by large numbers of commuters to get to stations and by housewives shopping in the local shopping districts. Because the roads are considered dangerous, most cyclists use footpaths; cycle paths are rare. Bicycles can be hired by the hour or day at most tourist centers, usually near the main station, and provide a convenient way to do sightseeing, cycle maps being provided.

The parts of a bicycle
(the diagram shows the numbered parts)

1	rear light	バック・ライト	*bakku right*
2	rear wheel	後車輪	*koh-sharin*
3	(luggage) carrier	荷台	*ni-digh*
4	bicycle fork	フォーク	*fohk*
5	bell	ベル	*beru*
	inner tube	チューブ	*choob*
	tire	タイヤ	*tigh-ya*
6	crank	クランク	*kurank*
7	gear change	変速機	*hen-soku-ki*
	wire	ワイヤー	*wigh-ya*
	generator	発電器	*hatsu-denki*
	frame	フレーム	*fraym*
8	dress guard	泥除け	*doro-yokay*
9	chain	チェーン	*chayn*
	chain guard	チェーン・カバー	*chayn kabah*
	odometer	走行距離計	*sohkoh kyohri-kay*
	child's seat	子供用いす	*kodomo-yoh isu*
10	headlight	ヘッドランプ	*heddo ramp*
	bulb	電球	*den-kyoo*
11	pedal	ペダル	*pedaru*
12	pump	空気入れ	*kooki-iray*
13	reflector	反射鏡	*hansha-kyoh*
14	brake shoe	ブレーキ・ブロック	*burayk-brok*
15	brake cable	ブレーキ・ケーブル	*burayk kayburu*
16	ring lock	キー	*kee*
17	carrier straps	荷台ロープ	*nidigh-rohp*
	tachometer	スピード・メーター	*speedo-mehtah*
18	spoke	スポーク	*spohk*
19	mudguard	泥よけ	*doro-yokay*
20	handlebar	ハンドル	*handoru*
21	chain wheel	チェーン・ホイール	*chayn hweeru*
	toe clip	トウクリップ	*toh-kuripp*
22	crank axle	クランク軸	*kurank-jiku*
	drum brake	ドラム・ブレーキ	*doram-burayk*
	rim	リム	*rimu*
23	valve	チューブ	*choob*
24	valve tube	タイヤバルブ	*tigh-ya barubu*
25	gear cable	ギア・ケーブル	*geeya kayburu*
26	fork	フォーク	*fohk*
27	front wheel	前車輪	*zen-sharin*
28	seat	サドル	*sadoru*

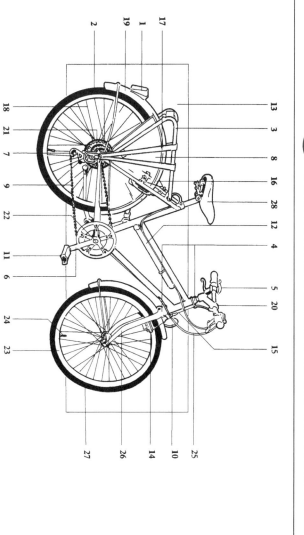

この自動車／自転車の部品はありません。	I don't have parts for your car/bicycle
部品はどこか他へ取りに行かなければなりません。	I have to get the parts from somewhere else
部品を注文しなければなりません。	I have to order the parts
半日かかります。	That'll take half a day
一日かかります。	That'll take a day
二、三日かかります。	That'll take a few days
一週間かかります。	That'll take a week
全損です。	Your car is a write-off
全然修理出来ません。	It can't be repaired
…時に自動車／バイク／オートバイ／自転車を取りに来れます。	The car/motorcycle/moped/bicycle will be ready at... o'clock

5 .8 Renting a vehicle

I'd like to rent a...	…を借りたいんですが。
	... o karitigh-n des-nga
Do I need a (special) licence for that?	(特別の)運転免許証がいりますか。
	(tokubets no) unten menkyoshoh-ga irimas-ka
I'd like to rent the... for...	…借りたいんですが。
	... kari-tigh-n-des-nga
– one day	一日
	ichi-nichi
– two days	二日
	futsuka
How much is that per day?	一日いくらですか?
	ichi-nichi ikura des-ka
– week?	一週間いくらですか?
	is-shookan ikura des-ka
How much is the deposit?	保証金はいくらですか?
	hoshoh-kin-wa ikura des-ka
Could I have a receipt for the deposit?	保証金の領収書お願いします。
	hoshoh-kin-no ryoh-shoo-sho o-negigh-shimas
How much is the surcharge per kilometer?	キロメートルにつき追加料金はいくらですか。
	kirometoru-ni-tsuki tsuika-ryohkin-wa ikura des-ka
Does that include gas?	ガソリン代は入っていますか。
	gasorin-digh-wa high-tay imas-ka
Does that include insurance?	保険は含まれていますか。
	hoken-wa fuku-maretay imas-ka
What time can I pick the...up tomorrow?	明日何時に取りにこれますか。
	ashta nanji-ni tori-ni koremas-ka
When does the...have to be back?	何時までに戻せばいいですか。
	nanji maday-ni modoseba ee des-ka

Where's the gas tank? _____	タンクはどこですか。
	tank-wa doko des-ka
What sort of fuel _____ does it take?	ガソリンは何ですか。
	gasorin-wa nan-des-ka

5.9 Hitchhiking

Hitchhiking is rare in Japan, but foreign tourists sometimes do it.

Where are you heading? ___	どこへ行きますか。
	doko-e ikimas-ka
Can I come along? _____	乗せて下さいますか。
	nosetay kudasa-e-mas-ka
Can my friend come too? _	友達も乗せて下さいますか。
	tomodachi-mo nosetay kudasa-e-mas-ka
I'm trying to get to..._____	…に行きたいんですが。
	... ni iki-tigh-n des-nga
Is that on the way to...? ____	…と同じ方角ですか。
	... to onaji hoh-gaku des-ka
Could you drop me off...? _	…で下ろして下さい。
	... de oroshtay kuda-sigh
– here? _____	ここ
	koko
– at the...exit? _____	…の出口
	... no deguchi
– in the center?_____	中心
	chooshin
– at the next intersection?_	次の交差点
	tsugi-no kohsaten
Could you stop here, please?	ここで止めて下さい。
	koko-de tometay kuda-sigh
I'd like to get out here _____	ここで下ろして下さい。
	koko-de oroshtay kuda-sigh
Thanks for the lift _____	ありがとうございました。
	arigatoh goza-imashta

Public transportation

6.1 In general

Where does this train go to?
この電車はどこへ行きますか。
kono densha-wa doko-e ikimas-ka

Does this boat go to...?
この船は…へ行きますか。
kono funay-wa ... e ikimas-ka

Can I take this bus to...?
このバスは…へ行きますか。
kono bas-wa ... e ikimas-ka

Does this train stop at...?
この電車は…に止まりますか。
kono densha-wa ... ni tomarimas-ka

Is this seat free?
この席は空いていますか。
kono seki-wa ightay imas-ka

– reserved?
これは指定席ですか。
kore-wa shtay-seki des-ka

I've reserved...
予約しました
yoyaku shimashta

Could you tell me where I have to get off for... ?
…へ行くには、どこで降りるか教えてください。
... e iku-ni-wa, doko-de oriru-ka oshi-etay kuda-sigh

Could you let me know when we get to...?
…に着いたら教えて下さい。
... ni tsui-tara oshi-etay kuda-sigh

Could you stop at the next stop, please?
次のバス停で下ろして下さい。
tsugi-no bas-tay-de oroshtay kuda-sigh

Where are we now?
今どのへんですか。
ima dono-hen des-ka

Do I have to get off here?
ここで降りなければなりませんか。
koko-de ori-nakereba-narimasen-ka

Have we already passed...?
もう…を通りましたか。
moh ... o tohri-mashta-ka

How long have I been asleep?
私はどのぐらい眠りましたか。
watasi-wa dono gurigh nemuri-mashta-ka

How long does...stop here?
…はここにどのくらい止まっていますか。
... wa koko-ni dono-kurigh tomattay imas-ka

Can I come back on the same ticket?
この切符は往復ですか。
kono kippu-wa ohf-ku des-ka

Can I change on this ticket?
この切符で乗り換えられますか。
kono kippu-de norikae-raremas-ka

How long is this ticket valid for?
この切符はいつまで有効ですか。
kono kippu-wa itsu maday yookoh des-ka

Ticket types

この切符は…ですか。	Is this ticket...?
一等	First class
二等	Second class
片道	One-way
往復	Round-trip
喫煙車	Smoking
禁煙車	No-smoking
窓側の座席	Window
通路側の座席	Aisle
列車の前方	Front
列車の後方	Back
座席	Seat
寝台車	Berth
上・中・下	Top, middle or bottom
エコノミークラスあるいはビジネスクラス?	Tourist class or business class?
船室あるいは座席?	Cabin or seat?
一人用あるいは二人用?	Single or double?
何人ですか。	How many are travelling?

Destination

どこへ行きますか。	Where are you travelling to?
いつ出発しますか。	When are you leaving?
…に出発します。	Your...leaves at...
乗り換えなければなりません。	You have to change trains
…で降りなければなりません。	You have to get off at...
…経由で行かなければなりません。	You have to travel via...
出発は…です。	The outward journey is on...
帰りは…です。	The return journey is on...
…までに乗船しなければなりません。	You have to be on board by...

Inside the vehicle

切符を見せて下さい。	Your ticket, please
指定席券を見せて下さい。	Your reservation, please
パスポートを見せて下さい。	Your passport, please
座席が違います。	You're in the wrong seat
違った…ですが。	You're on/in the wrong...
これは指定席です。	This seat is reserved
特別料金を払わなければなりません。	You'll have to pay an extra fare
…は…分遅れています。	The...has been delayed by...minutes

6.3 Tickets

Where can I buy a ticket?	切符はどこで買えますか。 *kipp-wa doko-de ka-emas-ka*
– make a reservation?	どこで予約出来ますか。 *doko-de yoyaku dekimas-ka*
– reserve a flight?	飛行機の切符はどこで買えますか。 *shikohki-no kippu-wa doko-de ka-emas-ka*
Could I have a one-way, please?	片道お願いします。 *katamichi onegigh-shimas*
– a round-trip?	往復お願いします。 *ohfuku onegigh-shimas*
first class	一等車 *ittoh-sha*
second class	二等車 *nitoh-sha*
tourist class	エコノミークラス *ekonomi-kurasu*
business class	ビジネスクラス *bijines-kuras*
I'd like to reserve a seat	座席を予約したいんです。 *zaseki-o yoyaku shitigh-n des*
– berth	寝台車を予約したいんです。 *shin-digh-sha-o yoyaku shitigh-n-des*
top/middle/bottom	上／中／下 *weh/naka/shta*
I'd like to reserve a cabin	船室を予約したいんです。 *senshits-o yoyaku shitigh-n des*
smoking/no smoking	喫煙／禁煙 *kitsu-en/kin(g)-en*
by the window	窓際で *mado-giwa-de*
single/double	一人用／二人用 *shtori-yoh/f-tari-yoh*
at the front/back of the train	列車の前方で／列車の後方で *ressha-no zempoh-de/ressha-no koh-hoh-de*
– of the plane	飛行機の前方で／飛行機の後方で *sh-kohki-no zempoh-de/sh-kohki-no koh-hoh-de*
One car	車は一台です。 *kuruma-wa ichi-digh des*
... bicycles	自転車は…台です。 *jitensha-wa ...digh des*
Do you also have season tickets?	定期券もありますか。 *tayki-ken-mo arimas-ka*

Public transportation

Where's...? — …はどこですか。
... wa doko des-ka

Where's the information desk? — 案内所はどこですか。
an-nigh-jo-wa doko des-ka

Where can I find a schedule? — 時刻表はどこですか。
jikoku-hyoh-wa doko des-ka

Where's the...desk? — …の売場はどこですか。
... no uriba-wa doko des-ka

Do you have a city map with the bus/the subway routes on it? — バスや地下鉄が載っている町の地図はありますか。
bas-ya chika-tets-ga nottay iru machi-no chizu-wa arimas-ka

Do you have a schedule? — 時刻表ありますか。
jikoku-hyoh arimas-ka

I'd like to confirm my reservation for/trip to... — …までの旅行／予約を確かめておきたいんです。
... maday-no ryokoh/yoyaku-o tashi-kametay oki-tigh-n des

I'd like to cancel my reservation for/trip to... — …までの旅行／予約を取り消したいんです。
... maday-no ryokoh/yoyaku-o torikeshi-tigh-n des

I'd like to change my reservation for/trip to... — …までの旅行／予約を変えたいんです。
... maday-no ryokoh/yoyaku-o ka-e-tigh-n des

Will I get my money back? — 払戻しを請求出来ますか。
ha-righ modoshi-o saykyoo dekimas-ka

I want to go to... How do I get there? (What's the quickest way there?) — …へ行きたいんですが、どのように行きますか（何が一番速いですか）。
... e iki-tigh-n des-nga, dono-yoh-ni ikimas-ka (nani-ga ichiban ha-yigh des-ka)

How much is a single to...? — …までの片道はいくらですか。
... maday-no katamichi-wa ikura des-ka

How much is a return to...? — …までの往復はいくらですか。
... maday-no ohf-ku-wa ikura des-ka

Do I have to pay extra? — 追加料金を払わなければなりませんか。
tswee-ka ryohkin-o harawa-nakereba-nari-masen-ka

Can I interrupt my journey with this ticket? — この切符で途中下車が出来ますか。
kono kippu-de tochoo gesha-ga dekimas-ka

How much luggage am I allowed? — 荷物は何キロまで持って行けますか。
nimots-wa nankiro-maday mottay ikemas-ka

Can I send my luggage in advance? — 荷物を宅急便で送れますか。
nimots-o takkyoo-bin-de okuremas-ka

Does this...travel direct? — この…は直行ですか。
kono ... wa chokkoh des-ka

Do I have to change? Where? — 乗り換えなければなりませんか。どこで
norikae-nakereba-narimasen-ka, doko-de

Will there be any stopovers? — 途中止まりますか。
tochoo tomarimas-ka

Does the boat call at any ports on the way?	途中港に寄港しますか。
	tochoo minato-ni kikoh shimas-ka
Does the train/bus stop at...?	この電車（バス）は…に止まりますか。
	kono densha (bas)-wa ... ni tomarimas-ka
Where should I get off?	どこで降りなければなりませんか。
	doko-de ori-nakereba-narimasen-ka
Is there a connection to...?	…までの接続はありますか。
	... maday-no setsu-zoku-wa arimas-ka
How long do I have to wait?	どのぐらい待たなければなりませんか。
	dono gurigh mata-nakereba-narimasen-ka
When does...leave?	…はいつ出発しますか。
	... wa its shuppats shimas-ka
What time does the next...leave?	次の…は何時に出発しますか。
	tsugi-no ....wa nanji-ni shuppats shimas-ka
What time does the last...leave?	最終の…は何時に出発しますか。
	sigh-shoo-no ... wa nanji-ni shuppats shimas-ka
How long does...take?	どのぐらいかかりますか。
	dono-gurigh kakarimas-ka
What time does... arrive in...?	…に何時に着きますか。
	... ni nanji-ni tsukimas-ka
Where does the...to... leave from?	…までの電車はどこから出発しますか。
	... maday-no densha-wa doko-kara shuppats shimas-ka
Is this the train/bus/ boat to...?	これは…までの電車／バス／船ですか。
	koray-wa ... maday-no densha/bas/funay des-ka

6 .5 Airport

到着	国際
arrivals	international
出発	国内
departures	domestic

● **The railway system in Japan is very well developed**, and managed by Japan Railways (JR) and a large number of private railway companies. Intercity trains are local (*futsoo*), express (*kyoo-koh*), limited express (*tokkyoo*), and super express (*shinkansen*).
Tickets are charged by distance, with surcharges for the category of train, class, and seat reservations. Ticket reservations are made at counters called "green windows" (*midori no madoguchi*). Tickets can be bought from ticket machines and most of these have an English option. The full fare does not have to be paid before the destination. Fare adjustment machines and counters are available. All JR stations show station names written in Japanese with the romanization below. Useful for travelers is the custom of including the names of the previous and next stations to the left and right underneath the station name.

.7 Taxis

● **Taxis are expensive, but all are metered and there is no custom of tipping.** Carry the address and phone number of your destination, and a map of the immediate location if possible, to give to the driver. Taxi doors are automated; normally the back curbside door is the only one used. On arrival, wait for the driver to open the door, and do not close it yourself.

空車 for hire	満車 booked	タクシー乗り場 taxi stand

Taxi _____	タクシー！ *tak-shee*
Could you get me a _____ taxi, please?	タクシーを呼んで下さい。 *tak-shee-o yonday kuda-sigh*
Where can I find a taxi ____ around here?	タクシー乗り場はどこですか。 *tak-shee noriba-wa doko des-ka*
Could you take me to..., ___ please?	…までお願いします。 *... maday o-negigh shimas*
– this address _____	この住所 *kono joosho*
– the...hotel _____	…ホテル *... hoteru*
– the town/city center_____	中心地 *choo-shin-chi*
– the station _____	駅 *eki*
– the airport_____	空港 *koo-koh*
How much is the _____ trip to...?	…までいくらですか。 *... maday ikura des-ka*

How far is it to...?	…まで何キロぐらいですか。	... maday nan-kiro gurigh des-ka
I'm in a hurry	急いでいるんですが	iso-iday irun des-nga
Could you speed up/ slow down a little?	もっと速く／ゆっくり行ってください。	motto hayaku/yukkuri ittay kuda-sigh
Could you take a different route?	他の道を取って下さい。	hoka-no michi-o tottay kuda-sigh
I'd like to get out here, please	ここで下ろして下さい。	koko-de oroshtay kuda-sigh
Here	ここで…	koko-de
You have to go straight on	…真っ直ぐ行ってください。	... massugu ittay kuda-sigh
You have to turn left	…左に曲がって下さい。	... hidari-ni magattay kuda-sigh
You have to turn right	…右に曲がって下さい。	... migi-ni magattay kuda-sigh
This is it	ここです。	koko des
Could you wait a minute for me, please?	ちょっと待ってて下さい。	chotto mattay-tay kuda-sigh

6

Public transportation

Overnight accommodation

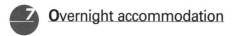

7 Overnight accommodation

7 .1 General

● **Japan has a great variety of overnight accommodation.** There is a wide range of hotels, from five-star international hotels to business hotels and small local establishments. The cheaper the hotel, the smaller the room and the fewer the facilities. Whatever the grade of hotel, cleanliness should be of high order. Other accommodation, especially in country areas, includes the very expensive luxury *ryokan* (traditional inns) and small, cheaper inns. Inns are a good way to experience the Japanese lifestyle. Rooms are covered with straw mats (*tatami*) and the guest sleeps on a mattress (*futon*) spread on the floor. In some inns meals (Japanese style) are also served in the room. Bathing is generally communal (men's and women's facilities are separated) in a large room containing a sunken bath (very hot) for relaxation and individual taps and stools to wash prior to entering the bath. In rural areas these baths may be *onsen* (hot springs).

Many small inns now operate as *minshuku*, inexpensive accommodation offering two meals. These can be booked through the travel counters at stations and airports. They are a good option especially when travelling in the country. In the last few years a western version called *pension* has also become popular. Camping is not popular, and campsites are few and poor in the way of facilities. Youth hostels, of which there is an extensive network, provide a cheap alternative.

いつまでお泊まりですか。	How long will you be staying?
この用紙に記入して下さい。	Fill in this form, please
パスポートをお願いします。	Could I see your passport?
保証金をお願いします。	I'll need a deposit
前払いでお願いします。	You'll have to pay in advance

My name's...I've made a reservation...	私は…です。部屋の予約をしてあります。 *watashi-wa ... des. heya-no yoyaku-o shtay arimas*
– over the phone	電話で *denwa-de*
– by mail	手紙で *tegami-de*
How much is it per night/week/ month?	一泊/一週間/一ヶ月はいくらですか。 *ippaku/isshookan/ikkagets-wa ikura des-ka*
We'll be staying at least two nights/two weeks	せめて二泊/二週間泊まりたいんですが。 *semetay nihaku/nishookan tomari-tigh-n-des-nga*
We don't know yet	まだ分かりませんが。 *mada wakarimasen-nga*
What time does the gate/door open?	何時に開きますか。 *nanji-ni akimas-ka*

61

– close?_____	何時に閉まりますか。
	nanji-ni shimarimas-ka
Could you get me a _____ taxi, please?	タクシーを呼んでくれませんか。
	takshee-o yonday kuremasen-ka
Is there any mail _____ for me?	私宛の手紙がありますか。
	watshi-atay-no tegami-ga arimas-ka

.2 Camping

See the diagram on page 65.

ご自分で場所を決めて下さい。 _____	You can pick your own site
場所が割り当てられています。 _____	You'll be allocated a site
あなたの場所の番号です。 _____	This is your site number
自動車に貼り付けて下さい。 _____	Stick this on your car, please
このカードをなくさないように。 _____	Please don't lose this card

Where's the manager?_____	管理人はどこですか。
	kanri-nin-wa doko des-ka
Are we allowed to _____ camp here?	ここでキャンプ出来ますか。
	koko-de kyamp dekimas-ka
There are...of us and..._____ tents	…人とテント…個です。
	...-nin to tento ...-ko des
Can we pick our own _____ site?	自分で場所を決めてもいいですか。
	jibun-de basho-o kimetay-mo ee des-ka
Do you have a quiet _____ spot for us?	静かな場所がありますか。
	shizuka-na basho-ga arimas-ka
Do you have any other _____ sites available?	他に場所がありませんか。
	hoka-ni basho-ga arimasen-ka
It's too windy/sunny/ _____ here	ここは風／日ざしが強過ぎます。
	koko-wa kazay/hizashi-ga tsuyo-sugi-mas
It's too shady here _____	ここは日陰が多過ぎます。
	koko-wa hikagay-ga oh-sugi-mas
It's too crowded here_____	ここは混み過ぎています。
	koko-wa komi-sugi-tay mas
The ground's too _____ hard/uneven	地面は堅過ぎます／でこぼこです
	jimen-wa kata-sugimas/deko-boko des
Do you have a level _____ spot for the camper/ trailer/folding trailer?	キャンピングカーのために平らな場所があります か。
	kyamping-kah-no tamay-ni tighra-na basho-ga arimas-ka
Could we have _____ adjoining sites?	一緒に立てられる場所がありますか。
	issho-ni tate-rareru basho-ga arimas-ka
Can we park the car _____ next to the tent?	テントの隣に駐車してもいいですか。
	tento-no tonari-ni choosha shtay-mo ee des-ka
How much is it per _____ person/tent/trailer/car?	一人／テント一個／キャンピングカー一台／ 車一台はいくらですか。
	shtori/tento ikko/kyamping-kah ichi-digh/ kuruma ichi-digh-wa ikura des-ka

---

Do you have any huts to rent?	貸小屋もありますか。
	kashi-goya-mo arimas-ka
Are there any...?	…ありますか。
	... arimas-ka
– any hot showers?	お湯のシャワー…
	oyu-no shawah
– washing machines?	洗濯機
	sentakki
Is there a...on the site?	キャンプ場に…ありますか。
	kyamp-jo-ni ... arimas-ka
Is there a children's play area on the site?	キャンプ場には、子供用の遊び場が ありますか。
	kyamp-jo-ni-wa kodomoyoh-no asobiba-ga arimas-ka
Can I rent a locker here?	ロッカーが借りられますか。
	rokkah-ga kari-raremas-ka
Are we allowed to barbecue here?	バーベキューをしてもいいですか。
	bahbekyoo-o shtay-mo ee des-ka
Are there any power outlets?	電気を使えますか。
	denki-o tsuka-emas-ka
Is there drinking water?	飲み水はありますか。
	nomi-mizu wa arimas-ka
When's the garbage collected?	ごみはいつ集めますか。
	gomi-wa its atsume-mas-ka
Do you sell gas bottles (butane gas/propane gas)?	ガスボンベはありますか。
	gas-bombay-wa arimas-ka

.3 Hotel/B&B/apartment/holiday rental

Do you have a single available?	一人部屋ありますか。
	shtori-beya arimas-ka
– double room...	二人部屋ありますか。
	ftari-beya arimas-ka
per person/per room	一人に付き／一部屋に付き
	shtori-ni-tski/ hito-heya-ni-tski
Does that include breakfast/lunch/dinner?	朝食／昼食／夕食付きですか。
	choh-shoku/choo-shoku/yoo-shoku tski-mas-ka
Could we have two adjoining rooms?	隣り合わせの部屋ありますか。
	tonari-awase-no heya arimas-ka
with toilet/bath/shower	トイレ／バス／シャワー付きの部屋
	toyray/bas/shawah-tski-no heya
without toilet/bath/ shower	トイレ／バス／シャワーなしの部屋
	toyray/bas/shawah-nashi-no heya
facing the street	道に面している部屋
	michi-ni men-shtay iru heya
not facing the street	道に面していない部屋
	michi-ni men-shtay i-nigh heya
with a view of the sea	海側の部屋
	umi-gawa-no heya
without a view of the sea	海に面していない部屋
	umi-ni men-shtay i-nigh heya
Is there an elevator in the hotel?	エレベーターありますか。
	erebehtah arimas-ka
Do you have room service?	ルームサービスありますか。
	room-sahbis arimas-ka
Could I see the room?	部屋を見せてもらえますか。
	heya-o misetay moraemas-ka

Camping equipment
(the diagram shows the numbered parts)

luggage space	荷物置場	*nimots-okiba*
can opener	かん切り	*kan-kiri*
butane gas bottle	ブタン・ガスボンベ	*butan-gas-bombay*
1 tool bag	自転車用バッグ	*jitensha-yoh baggu*
2 gas cooker	ガス・コンロ	*gas-konro*
3 groundsheet	グランドシート	*gurando sheeto*
hammer	かなづち	*kana-zuchi*
hammock	ハンモック	*hammok*
4 gas can	燃料タンク	*nenryoh-tank*
campfire	キャンプファイヤー	*kyamp figh-ya*
5 folding chair	折りたたみ式キャンプ用いす	*oritatami-shki kyamp-yoh isu*
6 insulated picnic box	クール・ボックス	*kooru bokks*
ice pack	アイスパック	*ighs-pakku*
compass	コンパス	*kompas*
wick	芯	*shin*
corkscrew	コルク栓抜き	*kork-sen-nuki*
7 airbed	エア・マットレス	*e-a mattres*
8 airbed plug	プラグ	*prag*
pump	空気入れ	*kooki iray*
9 awning	日よけ	*hi-yokay*
10 mat	マットレス	*mattres*
11 pan	鍋	*nabay*
12 pan handle	鍋つかみ	*nabay ts-kami*
primus stove	コンロ	*konro*
zip	ファスナー／ジッパー	*fasnah/ jippah*
13 backpack	リュックサック	*ryuk-sakk*
14 guy rope	張り網	*hari-zuna*
sleeping bag	寝袋	*ne-bukuro*
15 storm lantern	ランタン／灯油ランプ	*rantan/ toh-yoo ramp*
camp bed	キャンプ用ベッド	*kyamp-yoh beddo*
table	折りたたみ式（キャンプ用）テーブル	*oritatami-shki (kyamp-yoh) tayburu*
16 tent	テント	*tento*
17 tent peg	ペグ	*pegg*
18 tent pole	テント・ポール	*tento-pohru*
thermos	魔法瓶	*mahohbin*
19 water bottle	水筒	*sweetoh*
clothes hook	洗濯バサミ	*sentaku-basami*
clothes line	物干しロープ	*monohoshi rohp*
windbreak	風よけ	*kaze-yoke*
20 flashlight	懐中電灯／ポケットライト	*kigh-choo den-toh/pokett-righ-to*
pocket knife	小刀	*kogatana*

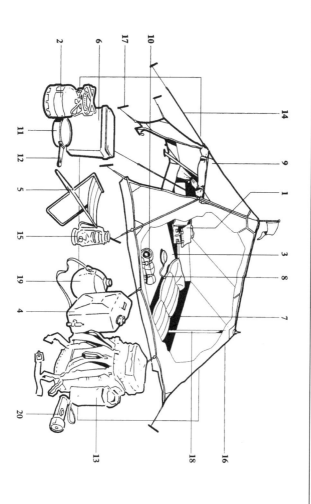

I'll take this room _____ この部屋に決めました。
kono-heya-ni kime-mashta

Please show us _____ 他の部屋を見せて下さい。
another room *hoka-no heya-o misetay kuda-sigh*

Do you have a larger _____ もっと大きい部屋はありませんか。
room? *motto ohkee heya-wa arimasen-ka*

Do you have a less _____ もっと安い部屋はありませんか。
expensive room? *motto yasui heya-wa arimasen-ka*

Could you put in a cot? _____ 子供用のベッドを追加できますか。
kodomo-yoh-no beddo-o tsweeka-dekimas-ka

What time's breakfast? _____ 朝食は何時ですか。
choh-shoku-wa nanji des-ka

トイレやバスは同階／部屋にあります。 _____ You can find the toilet and
shower on the same
floor/in the room

トイレやバスは部屋にあります。 _____ The toilet and shower are
in your room

こちらです。 _____ This way, please

…階にあります。 _____ Your room is on the...floor

部屋番号は…番です。 _____ Your room is number...

Where's the dining _____ 食堂はどこですか。
room? *shokudoh-wa doko des-ka*

Can I have breakfast _____ 朝食を部屋で食べられますか。
in my room? *choh-shoku-o heya-de tabe-rare-mas-ka*

Where's the emergency _____ 非常口はどこですか。
exit? *hijoh-guchi-wa doko des-ka*

– fire escape? _____ 非常階段はどこですか。
hijoh kigh-dan-wa doko des-ka

Where can I park _____ どこに駐車出来ますか。
my car? *doko-ni choo-sha dekimas-ka*

The key to room..., _____ …番の部屋の鍵お願いします。
please *...ban-no heya-no kagi o-negigh-shimas*

Could you put this _____ これを金庫に入れて下さいますか。
in the safe, please? *koray-o kinko-ni iretay kuda-sigh-mas-ka*

Could you wake me _____ 明日…時に起こして下さい。
at...tomorrow? *ashta ...ji-ni okoshtay kuda-sigh*

Could you find a _____ ベビーシッターがほしいんですが。
babysitter for me? *bebee-shitta-ga hoshee-n des-nga*

Could I have an extra _____ すみませんが、毛布もう一枚お願いします。
blanket? *sumimasen-nga, mofhu moh ichi-migh o-
negigh-shimas*

What days do the _____ お掃除は何曜日ですか。
cleaners come in? *osohji-wa nanyohbi des-ka*

When are the sheets/ _____ いつシーツ／タオルを取り替えますか。
towels changed? *its sheets/taoru-o tori-ka-emas-ka*

We can't sleep for _____ the noise	うるさくて眠れないんです。 *uru-sakutay nemure-nigh-n-des*
Could you turn the _____ radio down, please?	ラジオの音量を下げて下さい。 *rajio-no onryo-o sagetay kuda-sigh*
We're out of toilet _____ paper	トイレットペーパーがないんですが。 *toyretto-pehpah-ga naigh-n-des-nga*
There aren't any.../ _____ there's not enough...	…が足りないんです。 *... ga tari-nigh-n-des*
The bed linen's dirty_____	シーツがきたないのですが。 *sheets-ga kita-nigh-no-des-nga*
The room hasn't _____ been cleaned	部屋が掃除してありません。 *heya-ga sohji shtay arimasen*
The heater's not _____ working	暖房が働いていません。 *damboh-ga hatarigh-tay imasen*
The air conditioning's _____ not working	エアーコンが働いていません。 *e-a-kon-ga hatarigh-tay imasen*
There's no water _____	水が出ません。 *mizu-ga demasen*
– hot water _____	お湯が出ません。 *oyu-ga demasen*
– electricity _____	電気がありません。 *denki-ga arimasen*
...is broken_____	…がこわれています。 *... ga kowaretay imas*
Could you have that _____ seen to?	そのようによろしくお願いします。 *sono-yoh-ni yoroshku o-negigh-shimas*
Could I have another _____ room/site?	他の部屋に替えて下さい。 *hoka-no heya-ni ka-etay kuda-sigh*
The bed creaks terribly _____	ベッドがすごい音をたてるんですが。 *beddo-ga sugoi oto-o tateru-n-des-nga*
The bed sags _____	ベッドが柔らか過ぎます。 *beddo-ga yawaraka-sugimas*
There are bugs/insects _____ in our room	部屋に虫がいるんですが。 *heya-ni mushi-ga iru-n-des-nga*
This place is full of..._____	ここには…がたくさんいて、こまります。 *koko-ni-wa ... ga takusan itay, komarimas*
– mosquitos _____	蚊 *ka*
– cockroaches _____	ゴキブリ *go-kiburi*
– Americans _____	アメリカ人 *amerika-jin*

7 Overnight accommodation

7 .5 Departure

See also 8.2 Settling the bill

I'm leaving tomorrow. _____ Could I pay my bill, please?	明日立ちますから、精算して下さい。 *ashta tachi-mas-kara saysan shtay kuda-sigh*
What time should _____ we check out?	何時までに部屋をあけなければなりませんか。 *nanji maday-ni heya-o ake-nakereba-nari-masen-ka*
Could I have my _____ deposit/passport back, please?	保証金／パスポートを返して下さい。 *hoshoh-kin/paspohto-o kighshtay kuda-sigh*
We're in a terrible _____ hurry	大変急いでいます。 *tigh-hen isoi-de imas*
Could you forward my _____ mail to this address?	この住所に手紙を回送して下さいますか。 *kono joosho-ni tegami-o kighsoh shtay kuda-sigh-masu-ka*
Could we leave our _____ luggage here until we leave?	出発まで荷物をここに置いていてもいいですか。 *shuppats-maday nimots-o koko-ni oitay itay-mo ee des-ka*
Thanks for your _____ hospitality	おもてなしありがとうございました。 *omotenashi arigatoh go-zigh-mashta*

Overnight accommodation

7

Money matters

8 Money matters

● In general, banks are open Monday-Friday 9-3. They are closed on Saturdays, Sundays, and national holidays. Travelers' checks in yen or dollars are easily cashed at banks, but they are not readily acceptable outside the hotels and shops that cater particularly for the international traveler.

8.1 Banks

Where can I find a _____ bank/an exchange office around here?	この辺に銀行はありますか。 *kono-hen-ni ginkoh-wa arimas-ka*
Where can I find a _____ post office around here?	この辺に郵便局はありますか。 *kono-hen-ni yoobin-kyoku-wa arimas-ka*
Where can I cash this _____ traveler's check/giro check?	この (旅行用) 小切手はどこで現金に替えられますか。 *kono (ryokoh-yoh) kogit-tay-wa doko-de genkin-ni ka-eraremas-ka*
Can I cash this...here? _____	この…はここで現金に替えられますか。 *kono ... wa koko-de genkin-ni ka-eraremas-ka*
Can I withdraw money_____ on my credit card here?	クレジットカードで現金を引き出せますか。 *krejitto-kahdo-de genkin-o hiki-dasemas-ka*
What's the _____ minimum/maximum amount?	最小／最高はいくらですか。 *sigh-shoh/sigh-koh-wa ikura des-ka*
Can I take out less _____ than that?	少しでもいいですか。 *skoshi-demo ee des-ka*
I've had some money _____ transferred here. Has it arrived? These are the details of my bank in the U.S.	ここにお金を送金してもらいましたが、もう入金されていますか。これはイギリスの銀行の証書です。 *koko-ni o-kanay-o sohkin shtay morigh-mash-ta-nga, moh nyookin saretay imas-ka. koray-wa igirisu-no ginkoh no shoh-sho des*
This is my bank/giro _____ number	これは私の口座番号です。 *koray-wa watashi-no kohza bango des*
I'd like to change some ___ money	お金を両替したいんですが。 *okanay-o ryoh-gae shtigh-n des-nga*
– pounds into yen _____	ポンドを円に *pondo-o yen-ni*
– dollars into yen_____	ドルを円に *doru-o yen-ni*
What's the exchange _____ rate?	為替レートはいくらですか。 *kawasay rayto-wa ikura des-ka*
Could you give me _____ some small change with it?	こまかいお金も入れて下さい。 *komakigh okanay-mo iretay kuda-sigh*
This is not right _____	間違っていると思いますが *machigattay iru-to omoimas-ng*

ここに署名して下さい。____	Sign here, please	
これに記入して下さい。____	Fill this out, please	
パスポートを見せて下さい。____	Could I see your passport, please?	
身分証明書を見せて下さい。____	Could I see some identification, please?	
バンクカードを見せて下さい。____	Could I see your bank card, please?	

8 .2 Settling the bill

Could you put it on ____ my bill?	部屋に付けておいてください。
	heya-ni tsketay oitay kuda-sigh
Does this amount ____ include the tip?	サービス料は入っていますか。
	sahbis-ryoh-wa hight-tay imas-ka
Can I pay by...?____	…で払えますか。
	... de harae-mas-ka
– credit card? ____	クレジットカード
	krejitto-kahdo
– traveler's check? ____	旅行用小切手
	ryokoh-yoh kogit-tay
– with foreign currency? ___	外貨
	gigh-ka
You've given me ____ too much	おつりが多すぎます。
	otsuri-ga oh-sugimas
You haven't given me ____ enough change	おつりが少ないのですが。
	otsuri-ga sku-nigh des-nga
Could you check this ____ again, please?	もう一度確かめてくださいませんか。
	moh ichido tashi-kametay kuda-sigh-masen-ka
Could I have a receipt, ___ please?	領収書お願いします。
	ryoh-shoo-sho o-negigh-shimas
I don't have enough ____ money on me	すみませんが、持ち金が足りません。
	sumimasen-nga, mochi-ganay-nga tarimasen

クレジットカード／旅行用小切手／____ 外貨はご使用になれません。	We don't accept credit cards/traveler's checks/foreign currency

This is for you ____	どうぞ。
	dohzo
Keep the change ____	とっておいてください。
	tottay oitay kuda-sigh

Mail and telephone

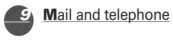

9 Mail and telephone

9 .1 Mail

● **Post offices open 9-5 Monday-Friday**, with cash-related facilities available until 3pm. The main offices in each ward are also open on Saturday mornings, 9-12:30. They are closed on Sundays and national holidays. However, they have after-hours services available for designated items, such as foreign mail. You must press the buzzer near the entrance and an attendant will come out to you. The Central Post Office across from Tokyo Station is open 24 hours a day. You can address letters using the English script (*romaji*).

郵便為替	電報
money orders	telegrams
郵便小包み	切手
parcels	stamps

Where's the post office/main post office?	この辺に郵便局(郵便局の本局)はありますか。 *kono-hen-ni yoo-bin-kyoku (yoo-bin-kyoku-no hon-kyoku)-wa arimas-ka*
Where's the mailbox?	この辺にポストはありますか。 *kono-hen-ni posto-wa arimas-ka*
Which counter should I go to...?	…はどの窓口ですか。 *... wa dono mado-guchi des-ka*
– to send a fax	ファックス *fakks*
– to change money	現金扱い *genkin ats-kigh*
– to change giro checks	小切手 *kogitay*
– for a Telegraph Money Order?	電信為替 *denshin kawasay*
General delivery	局留め *kyoku-domay*
Is there any mail for me? My name's...	私宛の郵便はありますか。私の名前は…です。 *watashi-atay-no yoobin-wa arimas-ka. watashi-no na-migh-wa ... des*

Stamps

What's the postage for a letter to...?	…までの手紙はいくらですか。 *... made-no tegami-wa ikura des-ka*
What's the postage for a postcard to...?	…までの葉書はいくらですか。 *... made-no hagaki-wa ikura des-ka*
Are there enough stamps on it?	切手は足りますか。 *kittay-wa tarimas-ka*
I'd like... ...yen stamps	…円の切手を…枚お願いします。 *...yen-no kittay-o ...migh onegigh-shimas*
I'd like to send this express.	これを速達便でお願いします。 *kore-o sokutats-bin-de o-negigh-shimas*

– by air mail _____	これを航空便でお願いします。
	kore-o kohkoobin-de o-negigh-shimas
– by registered mail _____	これを書留でお願いします。
	kore-o kaki-tomay-de o-negigh-shimas

Telegram/fax

I'd like to send a _____	…へ電報を送りたいんです。
telegram to...	*... e dempoh-o okuri-tigh-n des*
How much is that _____	一語につきいくらですか。
per word?	*ichigo-ni-tski ikura des-ka*
This is the text I _____	送る電文はこれです。
want to send.	*okuru denbun-wa koray des*
Shall I fill out the _____	用紙は自分で記入しましょうか。
form myself? ·	*yohshi-wa jibun-de kinyoo shimashoh-ka*
Can I make photocopies ___	ここでコピー出来ますか。
here?	*koko-de kopee dekimas-ka*
– send a fax here? _____	ここでファックス出来ますか。
	koko-de fakks dekimas-ka
How much is it per _____	一ページはいくらですか。
page?	*ippayji-wa ikura des-ka*

9 .2 Telephone

● **Dialing procedures are shown** by diagrams inside phone boxes.
Direct international calls can be made from card phones, most green
phones, and some grey ones. If a phone can be used to dial abroad,
the phone box will display a message in English to this effect.
However, owing to the abuse of telephone cards for international calls,
it may not be possible to use some card phones to dial overseas. The
basic unit-cost is 10 yen per minute. Fax machines are widely available.

To dial internationally through an operator, call 0051 (international
information service, 0057). Direct dialing is as follows: 001 – country
number – area code – local number. The national number of the US and
Canada is 1, Ireland 353, Australia 61, New Zealand 64, and UK 44. Omit
the 0 from the area code when dialing.

Could I use your _____	あなたの電話を使ってもいいですか。
phone, please?	*anata-no denwa-o tskattay mo ee des-ka*
Do you have a _____	電話帳ありますか。
(city/region)...phone	*denwa-choh arimas-ka*
directory?	
Could you find a _____	電話番号を調べて下さいませんか。
telephone number for	*denwa-bango-o shirabetay kudasa-i-masen-ka*
me?	
Where can I get a _____	テレホン・カードはどこで買えますか。
phone card?	*terehon-kahdo-wa doko-de ka-emas-ka*
Could you give me...? _____	…を教えてください。
	... o oshietay kuda-sigh
– the number of room... ___	…番の部屋の電話番号
	...ban-no heya-no denwa-bango
– the international _____	国際電話の番号
access code	*kok-sigh denwa-no bango*
– the country code for... ___	…の国番号
	... no kuni bango

– the area code for... ____	…の市外局番
	... no shi-gigh kyokuban
– the number of... _____	…の電話番号
	... no denwa-bango
Could you check if this ____ number's correct?	この電話番号が正しいかどうか調べて ください。
	kono denwa-bango-ga tada-shee-ka. dohka shirabetay kuda-sigh
Can I dial international ___ direct?	外国に直接ダイヤル出来ますか？
	gigh-koku-ni chokusetsu dighru dekimas-ka
Do I have to go through ___ the switchboard?	交換手を通してですか。
	kohkanshu-o tohsh-tay des-ka
Do I have to dial '0' first? __	最初にゼロをまわしますか。
	sigh-sho-ni zero-o mawashimas-ka
Do I have to reserve _____ my calls?	通話を申し込まなければなりませんか。
	tsoowa-o mohshi-koma-nakereba-narimasen-ka
Could you dial this _____ number for me, please?	この電話番号につないで下さい。
	kono denwa-bango-ni tsunigh-day kuda-sigh
Could you put me _____ through to.../extension..., please?	…番につないでください。
	...ban-ni tsunigh-day kuda-sigh
I'd like to place a _____ collect call to...	…にコレクトコールで電話をかけたいん ですが。
	...ni korekt-kohru-de denwa-o kake-tigh-n des-nga
What's the charge _____ per minute?	一分につきいくらですか。
	ippun-ni-tski ikura des-ka
Have there been any _____ calls for me?	私に電話がありましたか。
	watashi-ni denwa-ga arimashta-ka

The conversation

Hello, this is... _____	もしもし、…です。
	mosh moshi, ... des
Who is this, please? _____	どなたですか。
	donata des-ka
Is this...? _____	…さんですか。
	... san des-ka
I'm sorry, I've dialed the ___ wrong number	すみませんが、間違ってダイヤルしました。
	sumimasen-nga, machi-gattay dighru shimashta
I can't hear you _____	電話が遠くて、聞えにくいんですが。
	denwa-ga tohkutay, kikoe-nikui des-nga
Excuse me, I don't _____ speak Japanese	すみませんが、日本語が分かりません。
	sumimasen-ga, nihongo-ga wakarimasen
Is...there please? _____	…さんいらっしゃいますか。
	... san irasha-i-mas-ka
Is there anybody who ____ speaks English?	英語が出来る人いらっしゃいますか。
	aygo-ga dekiru shto irasha-i-mas-ka
Extension..., please _____	…番をお願いします。
	...ban-o o-ne-gigh shimas

Could you ask him/her _____ to call me back?	後で電話をしてくれるようお願いします。 *ato-de denwa-o shtay kureru-yoh o-ne-gigh shimas*
My name's... _____ My number's...	私の名前は…です。私の電話番号は…です。 *watashi-no na-migh-wa ... des. watashi-no denwa-bango-wa ... des*
Could you tell him/her _____ I called?	私が電話をかけたと伝えて下さい。 *watashi-wa denwa-o kaketa-to tsuta-etay kuda-sigh*
I'll call back tomorrow _____	明日また電話をかけます。 *ashta mata denwa-o kakemas*

電話です。 _____	There's a phone call for you
最初に0をダイヤルしてください。 _____	You have to dial '0' first
ちょっと待って下さい。 _____	One moment, please
通じません。 _____	There's no answer
話し中です。 _____	The line's busy
番号が違っています。 _____	You've got a wrong number
今留守です。 _____	He's/she's not here right now
…時に戻ります。 _____	He'll/she'll be back at...

Shopping

10 **S**hopping

● **Shops usually open around 10am and close around 8pm**.
Department stores close between 6pm and 7pm, depending on the
store and the day. All shops close one day per week. Neighborhood
shops, with the exception of supermarkets, tend to close on Sundays.
Large department stores are always open on Saturdays and Sundays,
but close for one day during the week except at busy times in July and
December. 'Convenience stores' which remain open 24 hours a day can
now be found in most urban localities. Discount stores offer
mainstream goods at up to 40% cheaper than the department stores.
There is a sales tax of 5% on all items; this is added to the final bill and
is not included in the price displayed. Bargaining is not the norm in
Japan, and attempts to do so will generally be met by a flat refusal. It is
customary for shop assistants to greet customers with the greeting
irasshaimase (welcome).

department store	デパート	*depahto*
antiques	骨董店／アンチーク	*kottoh-ten/ancheek*
household goods	雑貨屋	*zakka-ya*
camera shop	写真屋	*shashinya*
sports shop	スポーツ用品店	*spohts yoh-hin-ten*
second-hand goods	古物屋	*furumono-ya*
bicycle shop	自転車屋	*jitensha-ya*
liquor shop	酒屋	*sakaya*
shoe shop	靴屋	*kuts-ya*
butcher	肉屋	*nikuya*
shopping arcade	商店街	*shohten-gigh*
delicatessen	総菜屋／	*sohzigh-ya/*
	デリカテッセン	*derikatessen*
food shop	食料品店	*shokuryoh-hin-ten*
cake shop	ケーキ屋	*kayki-ya*
electrical appliances	電気屋	*denkiya*
tobacconist	タバコ屋	*tabakoya*
pharmacist	薬局	*yak-kyoku*
hardware shop	金物屋	*kanamono-ya*
florist	花屋	*hanaya*
grocery store	八百屋	*ya-oya*
greengrocer	果物屋	*kudamono-ya*
jeweler	貴金属店／宝石店	*kikinzoku-ten/hohseki-ten*
toy shop	おもちゃ屋	*omocha-ya*
laundry	洗濯屋	*sentaku-ya*
launderette	コインランドリー	*koyn rahnderee*
bookshop	本屋	*honya*
market	市場／マーケット	*ichiba/mahketto*
optician	眼鏡屋	*megane-ya*
bakery	パン屋	*panya*
beauty parlor	美容院	*biyoh-in*
hairdresser	床屋	*toko-ya*
perfume shop	香水店	*kohswee-ten*
fish market	魚屋	*sakana-ya*

kiosk	キオスク／売店	kiosk / bigh-ten
souvenir shop	みやげ物店	miyage-mono-ten
bicycle repairs	自転車屋	jitensha-ya
supermarket	スーパー	soopah
shop	店	misay
record shop	レコード屋	rekohdo-ya
leather shop	毛皮専門店	kegawa-semmon-ten
clothes shop	洋品店	yoh-hin-ten
dairy	牛乳屋	gyoo-nyoo-ya
china wear	瀬戸物屋	setomono-ya
candy shop	お菓子屋	okashi-ya
Do-it-yourself store	日曜大工店	nichiyoh-dighku-ten
dry cleaner	クリーニング屋	kureening-ya
fleamarket	のみの市	nomino-ichi
health food shop	健康食料品店	kenkoh-shokuryoh-hin-ten

🔟 .1 Shopping conversations

Where can I get...? ___
…はどの店にありますか。
... wa dono mise-ni arimas-ka

When does this shop ___
open?
この店はいつ開きますか。
kono mise-wa its akimas-ka

Could you tell me ___
where the...department is?
…売場はどこですか。
... uriba-wa doko des-ka

Could you help me, ___
please? I'm looking for...
すみませんが、…がほしいんですが。
sumimasen-nga, ... ga hoshee-n des-nga

Do you sell English/ ___
American newspapers?
英語の新聞もありますか。
eigo-no shimbun-mo arimas-ka

...please ___
…を下さい。
... o kuda-sigh

I'm just looking ___
ちょっと見ているだけです。
chotto mite-iru dakay des

I'd also like... ___
…も下さい。
... mo kuda-sigh

Could you show me...? ___
…を見せて下さい。
... o misetay kuda-sigh

Do you have ___
something...?
…のはありませんか。
... no-wa arimasen-ka

– less expensive? ___
もっと安い
motto ya-sui

– something smaller? ___
もっと小さい
motto chee-sigh

– something larger? ___
もっと大きい
motto oh-kee

I'll take this one ___
これ下さい。
koray kuda-sigh

Does it come with ___
instructions?
説明書は入っていますか。
setsumaysho-wa hight-tay imas-ka

It's too expensive ___
ちょっと高過ぎます。
chotto taka-sugimas

Could you keep this _____ for me? I'll come back for it later	あずかって下さいませんか。あとで取りに来ます。 *azukattay kudasa-i-masen-ka. ato-de tori-ni kimas*
Have you got a bag _____ for me, please?	ビニール袋ありますか。 *bineeru bukuro arimas-ka*
Could you gift wrap it, _____ please?	プレゼントですから、包んで下さい。 *prezento des-kara, ts-tsunday kuda-sigh*

すみませんが、ありません。 _____	I'm sorry, we don't have that
すみませんが、売切れです。 _____	I'm sorry, we're sold out
支払い所でお支払いください。 _____	You can pay at the cash desk
クレジットカードは使えません。 _____	We don't accept credit cards
旅行用小切手は使えません。 _____	We don't accept traveler's checks
外貨は使えません。 _____	We don't accept foreign currency

10 .2 Food

I'd like a hundred _____ grams of..., please	…を100グラムお願いします。 *... o hyaku gram o-negigh-shimas*
– five hundred grams/ _____ half a kilo of...	…を500グラム *... o gohyaku-gram*
– a kilo of... _____	…を1キロ *... o ichi-kiro*
Could you...it for me, _____ please?	…下さい。 *... kuda-sigh*
Could you slice it/chop _____ it for me, please?	薄く/さいの目に切って下さい。 *usuku/sigh-nomay-ni kittay kuda-sigh*
Could you grate it _____ for me, please?	おろしてください。 *oroshtay kuda-sigh*
Can I order it? _____	注文出来ますか。 *choomon dekimas-ka*
I'll pick it up _____ tomorrow/at...	あした/…時に取りに来ます。 *ashta/... ji-ni tori-ni kimas*
Can you eat this? _____	食べ物ですか。 *tabemono des-ka*
Can you drink this? _____	飲み物ですか。 *nomimono des-ka*
What's in it? _____	材料は何ですか。 *zigh-ryoh-wa nan des-ka*

I'd like something to go with this	何かこれに似合うのがほしいんですが。
	nani-ka kore-ni ni-au-no-ga hoshee-n des-nga
Do you have shoes to match this?	これに似合う靴がありますか。
	kore-ni ni-au kuts-ga arimas-ka
I'm a size...in the U.S.	イギリスの…サイズなんですが。
	igirisu-no ... sighz nan des-nga
Can I try this on?	試着出来ますか。
	shi-chaku dekimas-ka
Where's the fitting room?	試着室はどこですか。
	shi-chaku-shits-wa doko des-ka
It doesn't fit	このサイズは合いません。
	kono sighz-wa igh-masen
This is the right size	このサイズは大丈夫です。
	kono sighz-wa digh-johbu des
It doesn't suit me	似合いません。
	ni-igh imasen
The heel's too high/low	かかとが高過ぎます／低過ぎます。
	kakato-ga taka-sugimas / hiku-sugimas
Is this/are these genuine leather?	これは本当の皮ですか。
	kore-wa hontoh-no kawa des-ka
I'm looking for a...for a three-year-old child	3歳の子供のために…がほしいんですが。
	san-sigh-no kodomo-no tame-ni ... ga hoshee-n des-nga
I'd like a silk...	絹の…お願いします。
	kinu-no ... o-negigh shimas
– cotton...	木綿の…お願いします。
	momen-no ... o-negigh shimas
– woolen...	ウールの…お願いします。
	wooru-no ... o-negigh shimas
– linen...	麻の…お願いします。
	asa-no ... o-negigh shimas
What temperature can I wash it at?	洗濯温度は何度ですか。
	sentaku ondo-wa nando des-ka
Will it shrink in the wash?	洗ったら、縮みますか。
	arat-tara, chijimi-mas-ka

濡れたまま干して下さい。 Drip dry	洗濯機で洗えます。 Machine wash	アイロンをかけないで下さい。 Do not iron
手で洗って下さい。 Hand wash	ドライクリーニングにして下さい。 Dry clean	

At the cobbler

Could you mend these shoes?	この靴を修理出来ますか。
	kono kutsu-o, shoori dekimas-ka
Could you put new soles/heels on these?	新しい靴底／かかとを作ってください。
	atara-shee kuts-zoko/kakato-o ts-kuttay kuda-sigh
When will they be ready?	いつできますか。
	its dekimas-ka

I'd like..., please	…お願いします。
	... o-negigh shimas
– a tin of shoe polish	靴クリーム
	kuts-kreem
– a pair of shoelaces	靴ひも
	kutsu-himo

10 .4 Photographs and video

I'd like...	…下さい。
	... kuda-sigh
– a film	フィルム
	firum
– black and white film	黒白フィルム
	kuro-shiro firum
– color film	カラーフィルム
	karah-firum
– a slide film	スライドフィルム
	srighd-firum
– a cartridge	カセットフィルム
	kasetto-firum
– a videotape	ビデオテープ
	bideo-tehp
– an 8mm film	8 ミリ映画用フィルム
	hachi-miri ayga-yoh firum
12/24/36 exposures	12枚撮り／24枚撮り／36枚撮りのフィルム
	joo-ni-migh dori/nijoo-yon-migh dori/san
	joo-roku-migh dori no firum
ASA/DIN number	ASA/DIN 番号
	ay-ess-ay/dee-igh-en bango
daylight film	昼光用のフィルム
	chukoh-yoh-no firum
film for artificial light	人工光用のフィルム
	jinkohkoh-yoh-no firum

Problems

Could you load the film for me, please?	このカメラにフィルムを入れて下さい。
	kono kamera-ni firum-o iretay kuda-sigh
Could you take the film out for me, please?	フィルムを取り出して下さい。
	firum-o tori-dashtay kuda-sigh
Should I replace the batteries?	バッテリーを取り換えなければなりませんか。
	batteree-o tori-kae-nakereba-narimasen-ka
Could you have a look at my camera, please? It's not working	このカメラを見てくれませんか。使えなくなってしまいました。
	kono kamera-o mitay kuremasen-ka. tsuka-enaku-nattay shimaimashta
The...is broken	…がこわれました。
	... ga kowaremashta
The film's jammed	フィルムが動きません。
	firum-ga ugoki-masen
The film's broken	フィルムが切れました。
	firum-ga kiremashta
The flash isn't working	フラッシュが点灯しません。
	furash-ga tentoh shimasen

Processing and prints

I'd like to have this film developed, please	このフィルムを現像してください。 *kono firum-o genzoh shtay kuda-sigh*
– printed, please	このフィルムをプリントしてください。 *kono firum-o print shtay kuda-sigh*
I'd like...prints from each negative	このネガを…枚ずつプリントして下さい。 *kono nega-o ... migh-zuts print shtay kuda-sigh*
glossy/matte	光沢のある／光沢のない *kohtaku-no aru / kohtaku-no nigh*
I'd like to have this photo enlarged	これを引き伸ばして下さい。 *kore-o hiki-nobashtay kuda-sigh*
How much is...?	…はいくらですか。 *... wa ikura des-ka*
– processing?	現像 *genzoh*
– printing	プリント *print*
– the enlargement	引き伸ばし *hiki-nobashi*
When will they be ready?	いつできますか。 *its dekimas-ka*

10 .5 At the hairdresser's

Do I have to make an appointment?	予約しなければなりませんか。 *yoyak shi-nakereba narimasen-ka*
How long will I have to wait?	どのぐらい待ちますか。 *dono gurigh machimas-ka*
I'd like a...	髪を…下さい。 *kami-o ... kuda-sigh*
– shampoo	洗って *arattay*
– haircut	切って *kittay*
I'd like a shampoo for... please	…用のシャンプーお願いします。 *... yoh-no shampoo o-negigh shimas*
– oily hair	あぶらの多い髪 *abura-no oh-ee kami*
– dry hair	あぶらの少ない髪 *abura-no sku-nigh kami*
– a shampoo for permed hair	パーマをかけた髪 *pahm-o kaketa kami*
– a shampoo for colored hair	染まった髪 *somatta kami*
I'd like an anti-dandruff shampoo	ふけ防止用のシャンプーお願いします。 *f-kay bohshi-yoh-no shampoo o-negigh shimas*
– a color rinse shampoo	カラーシャンプーお願いします。 *karah shampoo o-negigh shimas*

I want to keep it the same color	この色と同じにして下さい。
	kono iro-to onaji-ni shtay kuda-sigh
I'd like it darker/lighter	もっと黒く／明るくして下さい。
	motto kuroku/akaruku shtay kuda-sigh
I'd like...	…をかけてください。
	... o kaketay kuda-sigh
I don't want...	…はかけないで下さい。
	... wa kake-nigh-day kuda-sigh
– hair spray	ヘアスプレー
	he-a spray
– gel	ジェル
	jeru
– lotion	ローション
	rohshon

I'd like short bangs	前髪を短く切って下さい。
	ma-e-gami-o miji-kaku kittay kuda-sigh
Not too short at the back	後は短過ぎないように
	ushiro-wa mijika-sugi-nigh yoh-ni
Not too long here	ここは長過ぎないように
	koko-wa naga-sugi-nigh yoh-ni
It needs a little taken off	少しだけ切って下さい。
	skoshi dakay kittay kuda-sigh
I want a completely different style	他の髪型にしたいんです。
	hoka-no kamigata-ni shitigh-n des
I'd like it the same...	…のような髪型にしたいんですが…
	... no yoh-na kamigata-ni shitigh-n des-nga
– as that lady's	あの方
	ano kata
– as in this photo	この写真
	kono shashin
Could you turn the drier up a bit?	ドライヤーを高くして下さい。
	drighyah-o takaku shtay kuda-sigh
Could you turn the drier down a bit?	ドライヤーを低くして下さい。
	drighyah-o hikuku shtay kuda-sigh
I'd like...	…をして下さい。
	... o shtay kuda-sigh
– a manicure	マニキュア
	manikyua
– a massage	マッサージ
	massahji

どんな髪型がいいんですか。	What style did you have in mind?
どんな色がいいんですか。	What color did you want it?
温度はよろしいですか。	Is the temperature all right for you?
雑誌をお読みになりますか。	Would you like something to read?
何かお飲みになりますか。	Would you like a drink?
これでよろしいですか。	Is this what you had in mind?

Could you trim... _____	…を切りそろえて下さい。
	... o kiri-soroetay kuda-sigh
– my bangs? _____	前髪
	ma-e-gami
– my beard? _____	ひげ
	higay
– my moustache? _____	口ひげ
	kuchi-higay
I'd like a shave, please_____	ひげを剃って下さい。
	hige-o sottay kuda-sigh
I'd like a wet shave, _____ please	ひげ剃り用カミソリで剃って下さい。
	hige-sori-yoh kamisori-de sottay kuda-sigh

Shopping

10

At the Tourist Information Center

At the Tourist Information Center

The Japan National Tourist Office (JNTO) provides information in English in Tokyo and Kyoto and at Narita Airport. There is also a Travel Phone service offering tourist information and language assistance in English during business hours. In smaller places, information centers are usually located at the railway station.

11 .1 **P**laces of interest

Most museums, tourist sites, and nationally famous temples and gardens charge entrance fees, which average around 400–600 yen for adults. If possible, wear shoes that can be slipped on and off easily, since many tourist attractions, particularly temples and old buildings, require shoes to be removed at the entrance.

Where's the Tourist Information center, please?	観光案内所はどこですか。 *kankoh an-nigh-sho-wa doko des-ka*
Do you have a city map?	町の地図ありますか。 *machi-no chizu arimas-ka*
Could you give me some information about...?	…について教えて下さい。 *... ni tsuitay oshietay kuda-sigh*
How much is that?	いくらですか。 *ikura des-ka*
What are the main places of interest?	主にどこが面白いですか。 *omo-ni doko-ga omoshiro-i des-ka*
Could you point them out on the map?	地図で指して下さい。 *chizu-de sashtay kuda-sigh*
What do you recommend?	何かおすすめは。 *nani-ka osusume-wa*
We'll be here...	ここに…います。 *koko-ni ... imas*
– for a few hours	二、三時間 *ni, san jikan*
– a day	一日 *ichi-nichi*
– a week	一週間 *is-shoo-kan*
We're interested in...	…に興味がありますが。 *... ni kyohmi-ga arimas-ga*
Is there a scenic walk around the city?	市内観光ありますか。 *shinigh kankoh arimas-ka*
How long does it take?	どのぐらい時間がかかりますか。 *dono gurigh jikan-ga kakarimas-ka*
Where does it start/end?	出発点／終点はどこですか。 *shuppats-ten/shooten-wa doko des-ka*
Are there any boat cruises here?	遊覧船がありますか。 *yooransen ga arimas-ka*
Where can we board?	どこで船に乗れますか。 *doko-de fune-ni noremas-ka*
Are there any bus tours?	観光バスがありますか。 *kankoh bas ga arimas-ka*

Where do we get on?	どこでバスに乗れますか。
	doko-de bas-ni noremas-ka
Is there a guide who speaks English?	英語のガイドがいますか。
	aygo-no gighd-ga imas-ka
What trips can we take around the area?	どこか楽しい小旅行はありますか。
	doko-ka tanoshee shoh-ryokoh-wa arimas-ka
Are there any excursions?	観光ツアーがありますか。
	kankoh-tsuah-ga arimas-ka
Where do they go to?	どこへ行きますか。
	doko-e ikimas-ka
We'd like to go to...	…へ行きたいんですが
	... e ikitigh-n des-nga
How long is the trip?	ツアーは何時間かかりますか。
	tsuah-wa nan-jikan kakarimas-ka
How long do we stay in...?	…にはどのくらい滞在しますか。
	... ni-wa dono kurigh tigh-zigh shimas-ka
Are there any guided tours?	ガイド付きツアーがありますか。
	gighd-tski-tsua-ga arimas-ka
How much free time will we have there?	どのくらい自由時間がありますか。
	dono-gurigh jiyoo jikan-ga arimas-ka
We want to go hiking	ハイキングに行きたいんですが。
	highking-ni iki-tigh-n des-nga
Can we hire a guide?	ガイドをたのめますか。
	gighd-o tanomemas-ka
Can I book mountain huts?	山小屋が予約出来ますか。
	yama-goya-ga yoyaku dekimas-ka
What time does...open?	何時に…が開きますか。
	nanji-ni ... ga akimas-ka
What time does...close?	何時に…が閉まりますか。
	nanji-ni ... ga shimarimas-ka
What days is...open?	何曜日に…が開いていますか。
	nanyohbi-ni ... ga igh-tay imas-ka
What days is...closed?	何曜日に…が閉まっていますか。
	nanyohbi-ni ... ga shimat-tay imas-ka
What's the admission price?	入場料はいくらですか。
	nyoojoh-ryoh-wa ikura des-ka
Is there...	…の割引切符ありますか。
	... no waribiki kippu arimas-ka
– a group discount?	グループ
	groop
– a child discount?	子供
	kodomo
– a discount for seniors?	65歳以上
	rokujoo-go-sigh ijoh
Can I take (flash) photos?	(フラッシュで) 写真を撮ってもいいですか。
	(frash-de) shashin-o totte-mo ee des-ka
Can I film here?	撮影してもいいですか。
	satsu-ay shtay-mo ee des-ka
Do you have any postcards of...?	…の絵葉書がありますか。
	... no eha-gaki-ga arimas-ka

Do you have an English...?	英語の…ありますか。
	aygo-no ... arimas-ka
– catalogue?	カタログ
	katarog
– program?	プログラム
	program
– brochure?	パンフレット
	panfretto

11 .2 Going out

Information about entertainment appears in the English language newspapers and in the visitors' guides which can be picked up in hotels. In Tokyo there is a Teletourist service which provides information about events and entertainment in English. Evening dress is rarely worn to the theater. Shows open earlier than in Europe, usually 6.30 or 7.00. Traditional theatre includes *Kabuki*, *No*, and *Bunraku*. Films generally are shown in the language of origin with Japanese subtitles.

Do you have this week's/month's entertainment guide?	今週／今月のプログラムありますか。
	konshoo / kongets-no program arimas-ka
What's on tonight?	今晩のプログラムはどうですか。
	komban-no program-wa doh des-ka
We want to go to...	…に行きたいんですが
	... ni ikitigh-n des-nga
Which films are showing?	どんな映画がありますか。
	donna ayga-ga arimas-ka
What sort of film is that?	どのような映画ですか。
	dono yoh-na ayga des-ka
rated adult (over 18)	成人映画
	sayjin ayga
original version	オリジナル版
	orijinaru-ban
subtitled	字幕付きで
	jimaku-tski-de
dubbed	吹替で
	fuki-kae-de
Is it a continuous showing?	繰り返し上演しますか。
	kuri-keashi joh-en shimas-ka
What's on at...?	何かいい…はありますか。
	nani-ka ee ... wa arimas-ka
– the theater?	ショー
	shoh
– the concert hall?	音楽会
	ongak-kigh
– the opera?	オペラ
	opera
Where can I find a good disco around here?	この辺にいいディスコはありますか。
	kono-hen-ni ee disko-wa arimas-ka
Is it members only?	会員だけですか。
	kigh-in-dakay des-ka
Where can I find a good nightclub around here?	この辺にいいナイト・クラブはありますか。
	kono-hen-ni ee night-krab-wa arimas-ka

Is it evening wear only? ___	正装は必要ですか。
	saysoh-wa hits-yoh des-ka
What time does the _____ show start?	ショーは何時からですか。
	shoh-wa nanji-kara des-ka

11 .3 Reserving tickets

Could you reserve...? _____	予約出来ますか。
	yoyaku dekimas-ka
– some tickets_____	切符
	kippu
– a seat in the orchestra ___	一階席で
	ik-kigh-seki-de
– a seat in the balcony_____	二階席で
	ni-kigh-seki-de
– box seats _____	ボックス席で
	boks-seki-de
– a table at the front_____	前方で
	zempoh-de
– in the middle _____	中ごろで
	naka-goro-de
– at the back _____	後方で
	koh-hoh-de
Could I reserve...seats ___ for the...o'clock performance?	…時の上演の切符を…枚予約出来ますか。
	... ji-no joh-en-no kippu-o ... migh yoyaku deki-mas-ka
Are there any seats _____ left for tonight?	今晩の切符はまだありますか。
	komban-no kippu-wa mada arimas-ka
How much is a ticket? _____	一枚いくらですか。
	ichimigh ikura des-ka
When can I pick the _____ tickets up?	切符はいつもらえますか。
	kippu-wa its morae-mas-ka
I've got a reservation _____	予約しました。
	yoyaku shimashta
My name's... _____	私の名前は…です。
	watashi-no na-migh-wa ... des

どの上演に予約したいんですか。 _____	Which performance do you want to reserve for?
どんな座席がほしいんですか。 _____	Where would you like to sit?
すみませんが、売切れです。 _____	Everything's sold out
立ち見席だけ残っています。 _____	It's standing room only
二階席だけ残っています。 _____	We've only got balcony seats left
一階席だけ残っています。 _____	We've only got orchestra seats left
前の座席が残っています。 _____	We've only got seats left at the front
後の座席が残っています。 _____	We've only got seats left at the back
何枚ですか。 _____	How many seats would you like?
…時までに切符を取りに来なければなりません。 _____	You'll have to pick up the tickets before...o'clock
切符を見せて下さい。 _____	Tickets, please
こちらの席です。 _____	This is your seat

Sports

12 Sports

The most popular spectator sports are baseball, soccer, and *sumo*. There are no public golf courses, but golf driving ranges are found in most places. Public tennis courts get very booked-up. Fitness and sports clubs are widespread.

12.1 Sporting questions

Where can we... around here?	この辺で…が出来ますか。
	kono-hen-de ... ga dekimas-ka
Is there a...around here?	この辺に…はありますか。
	kono-hen-ni ... wa arimas-ka
Can I hire a...here?	ここで…が借りられますか。
	kook-de ... ga kari-rare-mas-ka
Can I take...lessons?	…のレッスンが受けられますか。
	... no ressun-ga uke-rare-mas-ka
How much is that per hour/per day/a turn?	一時間／一日／一回いくらですか。
	ichi-jikan/ichinichi/ik-kigh ikura des-ka
Do I need a permit for that?	許可書が必要ですか。
	kyokasho-ga hits-yoh des-ka
Where can I get the permit?	許可書はどこで発行されますか。
	kyokasho-wa doko-de hak-koh saremas-ka

12.2 By the waterfront

Is it a long way to the sea still?	海岸までまだ遠いですか。
	kigh-gan maday mada toh-i des-ka
Is there a...around here?	この辺に…はありますか。
	kono hen-ni ... wa arimas-ka
– a swimming pool	プール
	pooru
– a sandy beach	砂浜
	sunahama
– mooring	埠頭
	f-toh
Are there any rocks here?	この辺には岩がありますか。
	kono-hen-ni-wa iwa-ga arimas-ka
When's high/low tide?	いつ満潮／干潮ですか。
	its manchoh/kanchoh des-ka
What's the water temperature?	水温は何度ですか。
	swee-on-wa nando des-ka
Is it (very) deep here?	（とても）深いですか。
	(totemo) fu-kigh des-ka
Can you stand here?	立てますか。
	tatemas-ka
Is it safe (for children) to swim here?	（子供が）安全に泳げますか。
	(kodomo-ga) anzen-ni oyogemas-ka
Are there any currents?	流れはきついですか。
	nagare-wa kitsui des-ka

Are there any rapids/ waterfalls in this river?	この川に急流／滝がありますか。	*kono kawa-ni kyooryoo/taki-ga arimas-ka*
What does that flag/ buoy mean?	あの旗／ブイはどういう意味ですか。	*ano hata/bui-wa doh yoo imi des-ka*

つり場	Fishing water
危険／注意	Danger
要許可書	Permits only
遊泳禁止	No swimming
サーフィン禁止	No surfing
つり禁止	No fishing

12 .3 In the snow

Can I take ski lessons here?	ここでスキーのレッスンが受けられますか。 *koko-de skee-ga naraemas-ka*
for beginners/advanced	初心者／上級 *shoshinsha / joh-kyoo*
How large are the groups?	グループは何人ぐらいですか。 *groop-wa nannin-gurigh des-ka*
What language are the classes in?	何語で教えられますか。 *nanigo-de oshie-raremas-ka*
I'd like a lift pass, please	リフトの一日券を下さい。 *rift-no ichinichi-ken-o kuda-sigh*
Must I give you a passport photo?	写真がいりますか。 *shashin-ga irimas-ka*
Where can I have a passport photo taken?	どこで写真を撮ってもらえますか。 *doko-de shashin-o tottay moraemas-ka*
Where are the beginners' slopes?	初心者のゲレンデはどこですか。 *shoshinsha no gerenday-wa doko des-ka*
Are there any runs for cross-country skiing?	この辺でクロスカントリースキーができますか。 *kono hen-de kros-kantree-skee-ga dekimas- ka*
Are the...in operation?	…は動いていますか。 *... wa ugoitay-imas-ka*
– ski lifts	スキーリフト *skeerift*
– chair lifts	リフト *rift*
Are the slopes usable?	ゲレンデは滑降可能ですか。 *gerenday-wa kakkoh kanoh des-ka*

Sports

12

Sickness

13 Sickness

English-speaking hospitals or clinics can be found in most large cities. Because of the high cost of medical and dental treatment, insurance is advised when travelling. There are pharmacies in every neighborhood and they are easily found.

13.1 Call (get) the doctor

Could you call/get a doctor quickly, please?
早くお医者さんを呼んで／連れてきて下さい。
hayaku o-isha-san-o yonday/tsretay-kitaykuda-sigh

When does the doctor ____ have office hours?
お医者さんの診察時間はいつですか。
o-isha-san-no shinsats- jikan-wa its des-ka

When can the doctor _____ come?
お医者さんはいつ来れますか。
o-isha-san-wa its koremas-ka

I'd like to make an _____ appointment to see the doctor
お医者さんの予約をして下さい。
o-isha-san-no yoyaku-o shtay kuda-sigh

I've got an appointment ___ to see the doctor at...
私は…時にお医者さんに会う約束があります。
watashi-wa ... ji-ni o-isha-san-ni au yakusoku-ga arimas

Which doctor (druggist) has night/weekend duty?
どの医者（薬局）が夜勤／週末勤務ですか。
dono isha (yak-kyoku)-ga yakin/shoomats kimmu des-ka

13.2 Patient's ailments

I don't feel well _____
具合が悪いんです。
gu-igh-ga waru-i-n des

I'm dizzy_____
めまいがします。
me-migh-ga shimas

– ill_____
病気です。
byohki des

– sick _____
気分が悪いんです。
kibun-ga waru-i-n des

I've got a cold_____
風邪です。
kazay des

It hurts here_____
ここが痛いんです。
koko-ga i-tigh-n des

I've been throwing up _____
もどしてしまったんです。
modoshtay shimatta-n des

I'm running a _____ temperature of...degrees
…度の熱があります。
... do-no nets-ga arimas

I've been stung _____
…に刺されました。
... ni sasare-mashta

– by a hornet _____
スズメバチ
suzume-bachi

– by an insect _____
虫
mushi

– by a jellyfish _____	クラゲ	
	kuragay	
I've been bitten _____	…に噛まれました。	
	... ni kamare-mashta	
– by a dog _____	犬	
	inu	
– by a snake _____	蛇	
	hebi	
– by an animal _____	動物	
	dohbuts	
I've cut myself _____	切り傷をつけました。	
	kiri-kizu-o tskemashta	
I've burned myself _____	やけどをしました。	
	yakedo-o shimashta	
I've grazed myself _____	肌をすりむきました。	
	hada-o suri-muki-mashta	
I've had a fall _____	ころびました。	
	korobimashta	
I've sprained my ankle_____	足首をくじきました。	
	ashi-kubi-o kujikimashta	

.3 The consultation

症状は何ですか。 _____	What seems to be the problem?
この症状はどのぐらい続いていますか。 ____	How long have you had these symptoms?
この症状は初めてですか。 _____	Have you had this trouble before?
熱は何度ですか。 _____	How high is your temperature?
脱いで下さい。 _____	Get undressed, please
上着を取って下さい。 _____	Strip to the waist, please
あそこで脱いでください。 _____	You can undress there
左／右腕をまくって下さい。 _____	Roll up your left/right sleeve, please
ここに横になって下さい。 _____	Lie down here, please
ここが痛いですか。 _____	Does this hurt?
深呼吸してください。 _____	Breathe deeply
口を開けて下さい。 _____	Open your mouth

Sickness

13

Patient's medical history

I'm a diabetic _____	糖尿病です。
	toh-nyoh-byoh des
I have a heart condition_____	心臓病です。
	shinzoh-byoh des
I have asthma_____	喘息病です。
	shinzoh-byoh des

I'm allergic to... _____	…に対してアレルギーです。
	... ni tigh-shtay arerugee des
I'm...months pregnant _____	…何ヶ月の妊娠です。
	... kagetsu-no ninshin des
I'm on a diet _____	食事制限をしています。
	shokuji saygen-o shtay imas
I'm on medication/ _____	薬／ピルを使っています。
the pill	*kusuri/piru-o tskattay imas*
I've had a heart attack _____	心臓麻痺をおこしたことがあります。
once before	*shinzoh mahi-o okoshta koto-ga arimas*
I've had a(n)...operation ___	…の手術を受けました。
	... no shujuts-o ukemashta
I've been ill recently _____	最近まで病気でした。
	sigh-kin maday byohki deshta
I've got an ulcer_____	潰瘍があります。
	kigh-yoh-ga arimas
I've got my period_____	月経です。
	gek-kay des

🖐

何かに対してアレルギーがありますか。 ____	Do you have any allergies?
薬を使っていますか。 _____	Are you on any
食事制限をしていますか。 _____	medication?
妊娠中ですか。 _____	Are you on a diet?
破傷風の予防接種をしましたか。 _____	Are you pregnant?
	Have you had a tetanus
	injection?

The diagnosis

🖐

深刻なものではありません。 _____	It's nothing serious
…が骨折しています。 _____	Your...is broken
…にあざがあります。 _____	You've got a/some
	bruised...
…をくじいています。 _____	You've got (a) torn...
炎症を起こしています。 _____	You've got an infection
虫垂炎を起こしています。 _____	You've got appendicitis
気管支炎を起こしています。 _____	You've got bronchitis
性病です。 _____	You've got a venereal
	disease
流行性感冒です。 _____	You've got the flu
心臓麻痺でした。 _____	You've had a heart attack
（ビールス／バクテリアに） _____	You've got an infection
感染しています。	(viral.../bacterial...)
肺炎です。 _____	You've got pneumonia
潰瘍があります。 _____	You've got an ulcer
筋をひきちがえました。 _____	You've pulled a muscle
膣の感染症です。 _____	You've got a vaginal
	infection

Sickness

13

98

食中毒です。 _____	You've got food poisoning
日射病です。 _____	You've got sunstroke
…に対してアレルギーがあります。 _____	You're allergic to...
妊娠です。 _____	You're pregnant
あなたの血液／小便／糞便を _____ 検査したいんです。	I'd like to have your blood/urine/stools tested
傷口を縫い合わせなければなりません。 ___	It needs stitches
専門医／病院に紹介します。 _____	I'm referring you to a specialist/sending you to the hospital
X線写真を撮らなければなりません。 _____	You'll need to have some x-rays taken
ちょっと待合室で待っていて下さい。 _____	Could you wait in the waiting room, please?
手術が必要です。 _____	You'll need an operation

Is it contagious? _____	伝染性ですか。 *densensay des-ka*
How long do I have _____ to stay...?	どのぐらい長く…にいなければなりませんか。 *dono gu-righ nagaku ... ni inakareba nari-masen-ka*
– in bed _____	ベッド *beddo*
– in the hospital _____	病院 *byoh-in*
Do I have to go on _____ a special diet?	食事制限をしなければなりませんか。 *shokuji saygen-o shinakereba narimasen-ka*
Am I allowed to travel? ___	旅行してもいいですか。 *ryokoh shtay-mo ee des-ka*
When do I have to _____ come back?	いつ伺わなければなりませんか。 *its ukagawa-nakereba narimasen-ka*
I'll come back tomorrow ___	また明日伺います。 *mata ashta uka-gigh-imas*

明日／…日後にここにきて下さい。_____	Come back tomorrow/ in...days' time

🔊 .4 Medication and prescriptions

How do I take this _____ medicine?	この薬はどう飲みますか。 *kono kusuri-wa doh nomimas-ka*
How many pills/ _____ drops/injections/spoonfuls /tablets each time?	一回どのくらいずつですか。 *ik-kigh dono-kurigh-zuts des-ka*
How many times a day? ___	一日何回ずつですか。 *ichinichi nankigh-zuts des-ka*
I've forgotten my _____ medication. At home I take...	薬を忘れてしまったんですが、普段は…を使っています。 *kusuri-o wasurete-shimatta-n-des-nga, foodan-wa ... o tskattay imas*
Could you write a _____ prescription for me?	処方を書いて下さいませんか。 *shohoh-o kaitay kudasa-i-masen-ka*

抗生物質／飲み薬／ トランキライザー／ 鎮痛剤の処方を書きます。	_____	I'm prescribing antibiotics/a mixture/a tranquillizer/pain killers
休まなければなりません。	_____	Have lots of rest
外へ出かけてはいけません。	_____	Stay indoors
寝ていなければなりません。	_____	Stay in bed

食事前に before meals	…日間 for...days	全部飲んで下さい swallow whole
カプセル capsules	注射 injections	錠剤 tablets
水に溶かす dissolve in water	外用のみ not for internal use	飲む take
ドロップ drops	軟膏 ointment	この薬は自動車の 　運転に影響を 　きたします。
…時間おきに every...hours	つける rub on	this medication impairs your driving
完全に治療を終 　わらせる finish the prescription	スプーン（大／小） spoonfuls (tablespoons/tea- spoons)	一日…回 ...times a day

13 .5 At the dentist's

Do you know a good _____ dentist?	いい歯医者を知っていますか。 *ee ha-isha-o shtay imas-ka*
Could you make _____ a dentist's appointment for me? It's urgent	私のために歯医者に予約して下さいませんか。急いでいます。 *watashi-no tame-ni ha-isha-ni yoyaku shtay kudasa-i-masen-ka. isoi-day imas*
Can I come in today, _____ please?	今日伺えますか。 *kyoh uka-gigh-emas-ka*
I have (terrible) _____ toothache	（すごく）歯が痛いんです。 *(sugoku) ha-ga i-tigh-n des*
Could you prescribe/ _____ give me a painkiller?	鎮痛剤の処方を書いて下さい／鎮痛剤をください。 *chintsoo-zigh-no shohoh-o kaitay kuda-sigh/chintsoo-zigh-o kuda-sigh*
A piece of my tooth _____ has broken off	歯がおれました。 *ha-ga oremashta*
My filling's come out _____	歯につめたのがとれました。 *ha-ni tsumeta-no-ga toremashta*
I've got a broken crown _____	歯冠がこわれました。 *shikan-ga koware-mashta*
I'd like a local _____ anaesthetic	局所麻酔をかけてください。 *kyokusho maswee-o kaketay kuda-sigh*
I don't want a local _____ anaesthetic	局所麻酔をかけないでください。 *kyokusho maswee-o kake-nigh-de kuda-sigh*

Can you do a temporary repair job?	応急治療をしてください。 *ohkyoo chiryo-o shtay kuda-sigh*
I don't want this tooth pulled	この歯は抜かないでください。 *kono ha-wa nuka-nigh-de kuda-sigh*
My dentures are _____ broken. Can you fix them?	入れ歯がこわれましたが、修理できますか。 *ireba-ga kowaremashta-ga, shoori dekimas-ka*

どの歯が痛いんですか。_____	Which tooth hurts?
はれています。_____	You've got an abscess
歯茎の治療が必要です。_____	I'll have to do a root canal
局所麻酔をかけます。_____	I'm giving you a local anaesthetic
この歯をつめなければ／抜かなければ／ けずらなければなりません。	I'll have to fill/pull this tooth/file this...down
穴を開けなければなりません。_____	I'll have to drill
口を大きく開けて下さい。_____	Open wide, please
口を閉めて下さい。_____	Close your mouth, please
口をゆすいで下さい。_____	Rinse, please
まだ痛いですか。_____	Does it hurt still?

Sickness

13

In trouble

14 In trouble

Emergency phone numbers: Police: 110; Ambulance/Fire: 119. On a public phone, press the red button and dial; no money is necessary. Speak slowly and clearly if there is no Japanese speaker with you. If you are in difficulty you can ring the Travel Phone service and speak to someone in English; insert 10 yen and dial 106 and in English say to the operator 'Collect call TIC'. The coin will be returned.

14 .1 Asking for help

Help!	助けて！
	tas-ketay!
Fire!	火事！
	kaji!
Police!	警察！
	kay-sats!
Quick!	早く！
	hayaku!
Danger!	危ない！
	abu-nigh!
Watch out!/Be careful!	あぶない！
	abu-nigh!
Stop!	止まれ！
	tomaray!
Don't!	しないで！／するな！
	shi-nigh-de! / suru-na!
Let go!	手をどけてよ！／手をはなして！
	te-o doketay yo! / te-o hanashtay!
Stop that thief!	泥棒を止めて！
	doroboh-o tometay!
Could you help me, please?	助けて下さい。
	tas-ketay kuda-sigh
Where's the police station/emergency exit/fire escape?	警察署／非常口／避難階段はどこですか。
	kaysats-sho/hijoh-guchi/hinan-kigh-dan-wa doko des-ka
Where's the fire extinguisher?	消火器はどこですか。
	shohkaki-wa doko-des-ka
Call the fire department!	消防車を呼んで！
	shohbohsha-o yonday!
Call the police!	警察を呼んで！
	kaysats-o yonday!
Call an ambulance!	救急車を呼んで！
	kyookyoosha-o yonday!
Where's the nearest phone?	電話はどこですか。
	denwa-wa doko des-ka
Could I use your phone?	電話を使わせてください。
	denwa-o ts-kawashtay kuda-sigh
What's the number for the police?	警察は何番ですか。
	kay-sats-wa namban des-ka

In trouble

14

14 .2 Loss

The railways, subway lines, and taxi companies have lost-and-found services.

I've lost my purse/_____ wallet
財布をなくしました。
sighfu-o naku-shimashta

I left my...yesterday_____
昨日…を置き忘れました。
kinoh ... o okiwasure-mashta

I left my...here_____
ここに…を置き忘れました。
koko-ni ... o oki-wasure-mashta

Did you find my...? _____
私の…が見つかりましたか。
watashi-no ... ga mitsukari-mashta-ka

It was right here_____
ここにありました。
koko-ni arimashta

It's quite valuable _____
とても貴重品です。
totemo kichoh-hin des

Where's the lost and _____ found property office?
忘れ物係りはどこですか。
wasuremono-kakari-wa doko des-ka

14 .3 Accidents

Robbery and violent crime are rare in Japan. The police maintain a visible presence through a network of small police stations called *koban*, usually found near railway stations. The policemen will help you find an address.

There's been an_____ accident
事故が起きました。
jiko-ga okimashta

Someone's fallen_____ into the water
人が水に落ちました。
shto-ga mizu-ni ochimashta

There's a fire_____
火事です。
kaji des

Is anyone hurt? _____
怪我をした人いますか。
kega-o shita shto imas-ka

Some people have _____ been injured
怪我人がいます。
keganin-ga imas

No one's been injured _____
怪我人はいません。
keganin-wa imasen

There's someone in _____ the car/train still
人がまだ車／列車に残っています。
shto-ga mada kuruma/ressha-ni nokottay imas

It's not too bad. _____ Don't worry
それほどでもありません。心配しないで下さい。
sore-hodo demo arimasen. shimpigh shi-nigh-de kuda-sigh

Leave everything the _____ way it is, please
何もさわらないで下さい。
nani-mo sawara-nigh-de kuda-sigh

I want to talk to the _____ police first
まず警察と話したいんです。
mazu kaysats-to hanashi-tigh-n des

I want to take a _____ photo first
まず写真を取りたいんです。
mazu shashin-o tori-tigh-n des

Here's my name and _____ address
これが私の名前と住所です。
kore-ga watashi-no na-migh-to joosho des

Could I have your _____ name and address?	あなたの名前と住所を教えて下さい。
	anata-no na-migh-to joosho-o oshietay kuda-sigh
Could I see some _____ identification/your insurance papers?	身分証明書／保険証書を見せて下さい。
	mibun shohmaysho/hokan-shohsho-o misetay kuda-sigh
Will you act as a _____ witness?	証人になってくれますか。
	shohnin-ni nattay kuremas-ka
I need the details _____ for the insurance	保険のために詳細が必要です。
	hoken-no tame-ni shoh-sigh-ga hits-yoh des
Are you insured? _____	保険に入っていますか。
	hoken-ni hight-tay imas-ka
Could you sign here, _____ please?	ここにサインをして下さい。
	koko-ni sign-o shtay kuda-sigh

🔴14 .4 Theft

I've been robbed _____	盗まれました。
	nusu-mare-mashta
My...has been stolen _____	…が盗まれました。
	... ga nusu-mare-mashta

🔴14 .5 Missing person

I've lost my child/ _____ grandmother	子供／祖母が迷子になりました。
	kodomo/sobo-ga mighgo-ni narimashta
Could you help me _____ find him/her?	捜すのを手伝って下さい。
	sagasu-no-o tetsudattay kuda-sigh
Have you seen a _____ small child?	小さい子を見ましたか。
	chee-sigh ko-o mimashta-ka
He's/she's...years old _____	…歳です。
	... sigh des
He's/she's got short/ _____ long/blond/red/brown/ black/gray/curly/straight/ frizzy hair	髪が短い／長い／金髪／赤い／茶色／黒い／白髪／巻き毛／真っ直ぐ／縮れ毛です。
	kami-ga miji-kigh/na-gigh/kimpats/a-kigh/cha-iro/kuro-i/hakuhats/maki-ge/mas-sugu/chijirege des
with a ponytail _____	ポニーテールで
	ponee-tehru des
with braids _____	三つ編みで
	mitsu-ami-de
in a bun _____	たばねて
	tabanetay
He's/she's got blue/ _____ brown eyes	目が青い…茶色です。
	me-ga ao-i ... cha-iro des
He's wearing _____ swimming trunks	海水パンツをはいています。
	kigh-swee pants-o high-tay imas
...hiking boots _____	登山靴をはいています。
	tohzan-gutsu-o high-tay imas
with glasses _____	眼鏡をかけています。
	meganay-o kaketay imas
tall/short _____	大きい／小さい
	oh-kee/chee-sigh
This is a photo of _____ him/her	彼…彼女の写真です。
	kare ... kanoji-no shashin des

In trouble

14

An arrest

運転免許証を見せて下さい。 _____	Your driving license, please
スピード違反です。 _____	
ここは駐車禁止です。 _____	You were speeding
	You're not allowed to park here
ライトがついていません。 _____	
罰金は…円です。 _____	Your lights aren't working
今払いますか。 _____	That's a...yen fine
今払わなければなりません。 _____	Do you want to pay now?
	You'll have to pay now

I don't speak _____ Japanese	日本語が話せません。 *nihongo-ga hanase-masen*
I didn't see the sign _____	あの交通標識が見えませんでした。 *ano kohtsoo-hyohshiki-ga miemasen deshta*
I don't understand _____ what it says	あの標識は分かりません。 *ano hyohshiki-wa wakarimasen*
I was only doing... _____ kilometers an hour	時速…キロだけで走っていました。 *jisoku ...kiro-dake-de hashittay imashta*
I'll have my car _____ checked	車を検査してもらいます。 *kuruma-o kensa shte-morigh-mas*
I was blinded by _____ oncoming lights	対向車のライトに目がくらみました。 *tigh-koh-sha-no righto-ni me-ga kurami-mashta*

At the police station

どこで起こりましたか。 _____	Where did it happen?
何をなくしましたか。 _____	What's missing?
何が盗まれましたか。 _____	What's been taken?
身分証明書を見せて下さい。 _____	Could I see some identification?
それは何時でしたか。 _____	What time did it happen?
誰が関係しましたか。 _____	Who was involved?
証人がいますか。 _____	Are there any witnesses?
ここに記入してください。 _____	Fill this out, please
ここにサインをして下さい。 _____	Sign here, please
通訳が必要ですか。 _____	Do you want an interpreter?

In trouble

14

I want to report a collision/missing person/rape	衝突／まい子／強姦を届けに来ました。 *shohtots/mighgo/gohkan-o todoke-ni kimashta*
Could you make out a report, please?	調書を書いて下さい。 *chohsho-o kigh-tay kuda-sigh*
Could I have a copy for the insurance?	保険のために写しをください。 *hoken-no tame-ni utsushi-o kuda-sigh*
I've lost everything	全部失いました。 *zembu ushi-nigh-mashta*
I've lost all my money	お金が全部なくなりました。 *okane-ga zembu nakunari-mashta*
Could you lend me some money?	お金を少し貸して下さいますか。 *okane-o skoshi kashtay kuda-sigh-mas-ka*
I'd like an interpreter	通訳が必要です。 *tsooyaku-ga hits-yoh des*
I'm innocent	私は無罪です。 *watashi-wa muzigh des*
I don't know anything about it	何も知りません。 *nan-ni-mo shirimasen*
I want to speak to someone	…の人と話したいんです。 *... no shto-to hanashi-tigh-n des*
...from the American consulate	アメリカ領事館 *amerika ryohjikan*
...from the American embassy	アメリカ大使館 *amerika tigh-shikan*
I want a lawyer who speaks English	英語が話せる弁護士がほしいんです。 *eigo ga hanaseru bengoshi-ga hoshee-n des*

In trouble

14

15

Word list

Word list English - Japanese

The following word list is meant to supplement the chapters in this book. Where the meaning of the word is very broad, notes have been inserted to show the sense in which the Japanese word is used. Some of the words not contained in this list can be found elsewhere in the book, e.g. alongside the diagrams of the car, bicycle and camping equipment.

A

100 grams	100グラム	hyaku-gram
a little	少し	skosh
about	約／だいたい	yaku/digh-tigh
above	上	ue
abroad	外国	gigh-kok
abundant	豊富な	hohfu-na
accident	事故	jiko
adder	マムシ	mamushi
addition	計算	kaysan
address	住所	joo-sho
admission	入場	nyoojoh
admission price	入場料	nyoojoh-ryoh
advice	忠告	choo-kok
after	…の後で	... no ato-de
afternoon	午後	gogo
aftershave	アフターシェーブローション	aftah-shayb rohshon
again	もう一度	moh ichido
against	…に対して	... ni tigh-shtay
age	年齢	nen-ray
AIDS	エイズ	ayz
air conditioning	エアコン	e-a-kon
air mattress	エア・マットレス	e-a mattoresu
airplane	飛行機	hikohki
airport	空港	kookoh
alarm	警告	kay-kok
alarm clock	目覚まし時計	mezamashi-dokay
alcohol	アルコール	aru-kohru
all the time	ずっと	zutto
allergic	アレルギー	areru-gee
alone	一人で	shtori day
always	いつも	its-mo
ambulance	救急車	kyoo-kyoo-sha
America	アメリカ	amerika
American	アメリカ人	amerika-jin
amount	総額	soh-gak
amusement park	遊園地	yoo-en-chi
anaesthetize (local)	局所麻酔をかける	kyokusho-maswee-o kakeru
anchovy	アンチョビー	anchobee
angry	おこった	okotta
animal	動物	doh-buts
ankle	くるぶし	kurubushi
answer	答え／返事	ko-tigh/henji
ant	アリ	ari
antibiotics	抗生物質	kohsay busshits
antifreeze	不凍液	f-toh-eki

antique	古代の	*kodigh-no*
antiques	古美術／骨董品	*kobijuts/kottoh-hin*
anus	肛門	*kohmon*
apartment	アパート	*a-pahto*
aperitif	食前酒	*shokuzen-shu*
apologies	許し	*yurushi*
apple	リンゴ	*ringo*
apple juice	リンゴジュース	*ringo joos*
apple pie	アップルパイ	*appuru pigh*
apple sauce	アップルソース	*appuru sohsu*
appointment	約束	*yak-soku*
apricot	アンズ	*anzu*
April	四月	*shigats*
architecture	建築	*ken-chiku*
area	環境	*kankyoh*
area code	市外局番	*shi-gigh kyokuban*
arm	腕	*uday*
arrange	約束する	*yak-soku suru*
arrive	着く	*tsuku*
arrow	矢印	*ya-jirushi*
art	芸術	*gay-juts*
artery	動脈	*doh-myaku*
article	物	*mono*
artificial respiration	人口呼吸	*jinkoh kokyoo*
ashtray	灰皿	*high-zara*
ask	尋ねる／問う	*tazuneru/tou*
ask (for)	頼む	*tanomu*
asparagus	アスパラガス	*asparagas*
aspirin	アスピリン	*aspirin*
assault	強姦	*gohkan*
at home	家に	*uchi-ni*
at night	夜	*yoru*
at the back	後に	*ushiro-ni*
at the front	前に	*ma-e-ni*
at the latest	遅くても	*osokutemo*
August	八月	*hachi-gats*
automatic	自動的	*jodoh-teki*
autumn	秋	*aki*
avalanche	雪崩	*nadaray*
awake	起きた	*okita*
awning	日よけ	*hiyokay*

B

baby	赤ちゃん	*aka-chan*
baby sitter	ベビーシッター	*baybee-shittah*
back	背中	*senaka*
backpack	リュックサック	*ryukkusakku*
bacon	ベーコン	*behkon*
bad	悪い	*waru-i*
bad (terrible)	ひどい／大変	*hidoi/tigh-hen*
bag	カバン	*kaban*
baker	パン屋	*pan-ya*
balcony	バルコニー	*barukonee*
ball	ボール／球	*bohru/tama*
ballet	バレー	*baray*
ballpoint pen	ボールペン	*bohru-pen*
banana	バナナ	*banana*

bandage	包帯	*hoh-tigh*
Bandaids	バンソウコウ	*bansohkoh*
bank	銀行	*gin-koh*
bangs	前髪	*ma-e-gami*
bank (river)	岸	*kishi*
bar (cafe)	バー	*bah*
bar	バー	*bah*
barbecue	バーベキュー	*bahbekyoo*
basketball (to play)	バスケットボール	*basketto-bohru*
bath	風呂／バス	*furo/bas*
bath towel	バスタオル	*bas-taoru*
bathing cap	海水帽	*kigh-swee boh*
bathing suit	水着	*mizu-gi*
bathroom	風呂場／バスルーム	*furoba/bas-room*
battery	バッテリー／電池	*betteree/denchi*
beach	浜／ビーチ	*hama/beechi*
beans	豆	*mamay*
beautiful	すばらしい／華美な	*subara-shee/kabi-na*
beautiful	美しい／きれいな	*utsuku-shee/kiray-na*
beauty parlor	美容院	*biyoh-in*
bed	ベッド／寝台	*beddo/shin-digh*
bee	ミツバチ	*mitsu-bachi*
beef	牛肉	*gyooniku*
beer	ビール	*beeru*
begin	始まる	*haji-maru*
beginner	初心者	*sho-shin-sha*
behind	後	*ushiro*
belt	ベルト	*beruto*
berth	寝台	*shin-digh*
better (to get)	元気になる／快復する	*genki-ni naru/kigh-fuku suru*
bicarb	重炭酸ソーダ	*jootan-san sohda*
bicycle	自転車	*jitensha*
bicycle pump	空気入れ	*kooki-iray*
bicycle repairman	自転車屋	*jitensha-ya*
bikini	ビキニ	*bikini*
bill	勘定	*kanjoh*
billiards (to play)	玉突きをする	*tama-tski-o suru*
birthday	誕生日	*tanjoh-bi*
biscuit	ビスケット／クッキー	*bisketto/kukkee*
bite	かむ	*kamu*
bitter	苦い	*ni-gigh*
black	黒い	*kuro-i*
bland (taste)	味のない	*aji-no nigh*
blanket	毛布	*mohf*
bleach	漂白する／脱色する	*hyoh-hak suru/dasshok suru*
blister	水膨れ	*mizu-buku-ray*
blond	金髪	*kimpats*
blood	血液	*kets-eki*
blood pressure	血圧	*kets-ats*
bloody nose	鼻血	*hana-ji*
blouse	ブラウス	*burausu*
blow dry	ブロー・ドライ	*buroh-drigh*
blue	青い	*a-oi*
blunt	鈍い	*nibui*
boat	ボート	*bohto*

Word list

15

body	体	karada
boiled	茹でた	yudeta
boiled ham	ハム	hamu
bonbon	ボンボン	bonbon
bone	骨	honay
bonnet	ボンネット	bon-netto
book	本	hon
booked (theater ticket)	予約した	yoyaku shta
booking office (theater ticket)	プレーガイド	pureh-gighdo
bookshop	本屋	hon-ya
border	国境	kokkyoh
bored (to be)	飽きた	akita
boring	面白くない／つまらない	omoshi-roku-nigh/tsumara-nigh
born	生まれた	umareta
borrow (from)	…から借りる	... kara kariru
botanical gardens	植物園	shokubutsu-en
both	両方	ryoh-hoh
bottle	びん	bin
bottle (baby's)	哺乳びん	honyoo-bin
bottle-warmer	哺乳びん保温器	honyoo-bin ho-onki
bowling	ボーリングをする	bohring-o suru
box	箱	hako
box office	プレーガイド	pureh-gighdo
box (in theater)	ボックス席で	bokks-seki-de
boy	男の子	otoko-no ko
bra	ブラジャー	burajah
bracelet	腕輪／ブレスレット	uday-wa/bures-retto
braised	煮込んだ	nikonda
brake	ブレーキ	brayki
brake oil	ブレーキオイル	brayki-oiru
bread	パン	pan
break	折る	oru
breakfast	朝ご飯	asa-gohan
breast	胸	munay
breast milk	母乳	bonyu
bridge	橋	hashi
briefs	パンツ／パンティー	pants/pantee
bring	持ってくる	mottay kuru
brochure	パンフレット	panfretto
broken	破れた／こわれた	yabureta/kowareta
brother (older, other's)	お兄さん	o-nee-san
brother (older, own)	兄	ani
brother (younger, other's)	弟さん	o-tohto-san
brother (younger, own)	弟	o-tohto
brown	茶色	cha-iro
bruise	あざができる	aza-ga dekiru
brush	ブラシ	burashi
Brussels sprouts	芽キャベツ	me-kyabets
bucket	バケツ	baketsu
bugs	害虫／ばい菌	gigh-choo/bigh-kin
building	建物	tate-mono
bun	菓子パン	kashi-pan
buoy	ブイ	bui
burglary	押し込み	oshikomi
burn	火傷	yakedo

burn (verb)	やける	*yakeru*
burnt	焼いた	*yigh-ta*
bus	バス	*bas*
bus station	バスの発着所	*bas-no hachaku-jo*
bus stop	バス停	*bas-tay*
business class	ビジネスクラス	*bijinesu-kuras*
business trip	出張	*shutchoh*
busy (schedule)	忙しい	*isogashee*
busy (traffic)	混雑	*konzats*
butane camping gas	ブタン・ガス	*butan-gas*
butcher	肉屋	*niku-ya*
butter	バター	*batah*
button	ボタン	*botan*
buy	買う	*ka-u*
by airmail	航空便で	*kohkoobin-de*
by phone	電話で	*denwa-de*

c

cabbage	キャベツ	*kyabets*
cabin	船室	*sen-shits*
cake	ケーキ	*kehki*
cake shop	ケーキ屋／お菓子屋	*kayki-ya/okashi-ya*
call	呼び出し	*yobi-dashi*
call (phone)	電話をする	*denwa-o suru*
called (name)	…と言う／…と言います	*... to yoo/... to eemas*
camera	カメラ	*kamera*
camp (verb)	キャンプする	*kyampu suru*
camp shop	キャンプ場売店	*kyampu-jo bigh-ten*
camp site	キャンプ場	*kyampu-jo*
camper	キャンピングカー	*kyamping-kah*
campfire	キャンプファイヤー	*kyampu-figh-yah*
camping guide	キャンプ案内	*kyampu an-nigh*
camping permit	キャンプ場使用許可書	*kyampu-jo shiyoh kyoka-sho*
cancel	取り消す	*tori-kes*
candle	ローソク	*rohsok*
candy	お菓子／おやつ	*okashi/oyats*
canoe	カヌー	*ka-noo*
canoe (verb)	カヌーをこいで行く	*ka-noo-o ko-iday iku*
car	車／自動車	*kuruma/jidoh-sha*
car deck	自動車用の甲板	*jidoh-sha-yohno kampan*
car documents	車の証明書	*kuruma-no shohmay-sho*
car seat (child's)	ベビーシート	*bebee sheeto*
car trouble	車の故障	*kuruma-no koshoh*
caravan	キャラバン	*kyaraban*
cardigan	カーディガン	*kahdigan*
careful	注意深い	*choo-i-bu-kigh*
carrot	にんじん	*ninjin*
carriage	乳母車／ベビーカー	*ubaguruma/baybee-kah*
cartridge	カセットフィルム	*kasetto-firum*
cascade	滝	*taki*
cash desk	支払い所	*shi-harigh-jo*
casino	カジノ	*kajino*
cassette	カセット・テープ	*kasetto-tayp*

castle	城	shiro
cat	猫	neko
catalogue	カタログ	katarog
cathedral	大聖堂	digh-say-doh
cauliflower	カリフラワー	kari-fura-wah
cave	ほら穴	hora-ana
CD	シーディー	shee-dee
celebrate	祝う	iwau
cemetery	墓地	bochi
centimeter	センチ（メートル）	senchi (mehtoru)
central heating	セントラル・ヒーティング	sentoraru-heetingu
center	…の中の	... no naka-no
center (city)	中心地	choo-shin-chi
chair	椅子	isu
chambermaid	ルーム係り	room-gakari
champagne	シャンペン	shanpen
change	変える	kaeru
change (money)	両替	ryoh-gigh
change (money) (verb)	両替する	ryoh-gigh suru
change (trains)	乗り換える	nori-ka-eru
change the baby's diaper	おむつを取り替える	omutsu-o tori-ka-eru
change the oil	オイルを交換する	oiru-o kohkan suru
charter flight	チャーター便	chahtah-bin
chat	言い寄る	ee-yoru
checked luggage	手荷物一時預かり所	te-nimots ichi-ji azukari-jo
check	チェッカー	chekkah
cheers	乾杯	kam-pigh
cheese	チーズ	cheez
chef	コックさん	kukku-san
check	小切手	kogit-tay
cherries	チェリー／サクランボ	cheree/sakurambo
chess (to play)	チェスをする	chesu-o suru
chewing gum	チューインガム	chooing-gam
chicken	ニワトリ	niwatori
child (other's)	お子さん	okosan
child (own)	子供	kodomo
child's seat	子供用いす	kodomo-yoh isu
chilled	冷たくした	tsumetaku shta
chin	あご	ago
chocolate	チョコレート	choko-rehto
choose	選択する／選ぶ	sentaku suru/erabu
chop (with breadcrumb)	カツレツ	katsuretsu
chop (meat)	挽き肉	hiki-niku
church	教会	kyoh-kigh
church service	礼拝	ray-high
cigar	葉巻	hamaki
cigar shop	たばこ屋	tabakoya
cigarette	たばこ	tabako
circle	円	en
circus	サーカス	sahkas
city	市	shi
clean	清潔な	sayketsu-na
clean (verb)	掃除する	sohji suru
clear	はっきりした	hakkiri shta
clearance (sale)	セール	sayru

clock	時計	*to-kay*
closed	閉まっている	*shmatte-iru*
closed off (road)	通行止め	*tsoo-koh domay*
clothes	衣服	*if-ku*
clothes hanger	ハンガー／衣紋掛け	*han-gah/emon-kakay*
clothes pin	洗濯ばさみ	*sentaku-basami*
clothing	衣類	*i-rui*
coat	コート	*kohto*
cockroach	ゴキブリ／アブラムシ	*gokiburi/abura-mushi*
cocoa	ココア	*koko-a*
cod	タラ	*tara*
coffee	コーヒー	*koh-hee*
coffee filter	コーヒー・フィルター	*koh-hee firutah*
cognac	コニャック	*konnyakku*
cold	風邪	*kazay*
cold (not hot)	寒い	*samu-i*
collarbone	鎖骨	*sakots*
colleague	同僚	*doh-ryoh*
collision	衝突	*shoh-tots*
cologne	化粧水	*keshoh-swee*
color	色	*iro*
color pencils	色鉛筆	*iro-empits*
color television	カラーテレビ	*karah-terebi*
coloring book	ぬり絵の本	*nuri-e-no hon*
comb	くし	*kushi*
come	来る	*kuru*
come back	戻って来る	*modottay kuru*
compartment	コンパートメント	*konpahtomento*
complaint	苦情	*kujoh*
complaint (illness)	痛み	*itami*
completely	全く	*mattaku*
compliment	賛辞	*sanji*
compulsory	義務	*gimu*
concert (classical)	コンサート	*konsahto*
concert hall	コンサートホール	*konsahto-hohru*
concussion	脳しんとう	*noh-shintoh*
condensed milk	クリーム	*kureem*
condom	コンドーム	*kondohm*
congratulate	祝う	*iwa-u*
connection	接続	*setsu-zoku*
constipation	便秘	*bempi*
consulate	領事館	*ryohji-kan*
consultation (house call by doctor)	往診	*ohshin*
contact lens	コンタクトレンズ	*kontakuto-renzu*
contagious	伝染性の	*densensay-no*
contraceptive	避妊の	*hinin-no*
contraceptive pill	避妊薬／ピル	*hinin-yak/piru*
cook	コック	*kokku*
cook (verb)	料理する	*ryohri suru*
copper	銅	*doh*
copy	コピー	*kopee*
corkscrew	コルク栓抜き	*koruk-sen-nuki*
corn flour	コーンスターチ	*kohn-stahchi*
corner	隅／角	*sumi/kado*

Word list

15

correct	正しい	tada-shee
correspond	文通する	bun-tsoo suru
corridor	廊下	rohka
costume	衣装	i-shoh
cot	ベビーベッド	bebee-beddo
cotton	木綿	momen
cotton antiseptic	脱脂綿／綿	dasshi-men/wata
cough	咳	seki
cough (verb)	咳込む	seki-komu
cough syrup	咳止めシロップ	seki-domay shiroppu
counter	受付け	uke-tskay
country (nation)	国	kuni
country (rural area)	田舎	inaka
country code	国番号	kuni ban-go
course (of treatment)	治療	chi-ryoh
cousin	いとこ	itoko
crab	蟹	kani
cream	クリーム	kureem
cream (fresh)	生クリーム	nama-kureemu
credit card	クレジット・カード	kurejitto-kahdo
croissant	クロワッサン	kuro-wasson
cross the road	横断する	ohdan suru
cross-country run	クロスカントリー スキー用のコース	kuros-kantoree-skee-yoh no kohs
cross-country skiing	クロスカントリー スキー	kuros-kantoree-skee
cross-country skis	クロスカントリー用 スキー	kuros-kantoreeyoh-skee
cry	泣く	naku
cubic meter	立方メートル	rippoh mehtoru
cucumber	キュウリ	kyoori
cuddly toy	ぬいぐるみ	nui-gurumi
cuff links	カフス・ボタン	kafs-botan
culottes	キュロット	kyoo-rotto
cup	茶わん	chawan
curly	巻き毛の	maki-ge-no
current	流れ／電流	nagaray/denryuh
cushion	クッション	kusshon
customary	普通／いつも	futsoo/itsumo
customs	税関	zaykan
cut	切る	kiru
cutlery	ナイフとフォークと スプーン	nighf-to fohk-to spoon
cycling	サイクリング	sigh-kuringu

D

dairy products	乳製品	nyoo-say-hin
damage	損害	son-gigh
dance	踊る	odoru
dandruff	ふけ	f-kay
danger	危険	kiken
dangerous	危険な	kiken-na
dark	暗い	ku-righ
date	デート	dayto
daughter (other's)	娘さん	musu-may-san
daughter (own)	娘	musu-may
day	日	hi

day (the whole)	まる一日	*maru ichinichi*
day before yesterday	一昨日	*ototoi*
dead	亡くなった	*nakunatta*
decaffeinated	カフェインなし／	*kafayn-nashi/*
	カフェインフリー	*kafayn-free*
December	十二月	*joo-ni-gats*
deck chair	ビーチ・チェアー	*beechi-cheyah*
declare (customs)	申告する	*shin-koku suru*
deep	深い	*fu-kigh*
deep sea diving	スキンダイビング	*skin-dighbingu*
deep freeze	冷凍庫	*raytohko*
degrees	度	*do*
delay	停滞／遅延	*tay-tigh/chi-en*
delicious	おいしい	*o-ishee*
dentist	歯医者	*ha-isha*
dentures	入れ歯	*ireba*
deodorant	デオドラント	*deodoranto*
department	部	*bu*
department store	デパート	*depahto*
departure	出発	*shuppats*
departure time	出発時間	*shuppats jikan*
depilatory cream	脱毛クリーム	*datsumoh-kreem*
deposit	手付け金／頭金	*te-tsuke-kin/atama-kin*
deposit (for safekeeping)	保管	*hokan*
dessert	デザート	*dezahto*
destination	行き先	*yuki-saki*
destination (terminal)	終点	*shooten*
develop (photo)	現像する	*genzoh suru*
diabetic	糖尿病患者	*toh-nyoh-byoh kanja*
dial	ダイヤル	*digh-yaru*
diamond	ダイヤモンド	*digh-a-mondo*
diaper	おしめ	*o-shimay*
diarrhea	下痢	*geri*
dictionary	辞典	*jiten*
diesel/diesel oil	ディーゼル	*deezeru*
diet	ダイエット	*digh-etto*
difficulty	困難	*kon-nan*
dining room	食堂	*shoku-doh*
dining/buffet car	食堂車／	*shokudoh-sha/*
	ビュッフェカー	*buffay-kah*
dinner	ディナー	*dinah*
dinner (to have)	ディナーを食べる	*dinah-o taberu*
dinner jacket	ディナー用ジャケット	*dinah-yoh jaketto*
direction	方向	*hohkoh*
directly	直接に	*choku-setsu-ni*
dirty	きたない／汚れた	*kita-nigh/yogoreta*
disabled	障害者	*shoh-gigh-sha*
disco	ディスコ	*disko*
discount	割引	*wari-biki*
dish	一皿／一品	*shto-sara/ippin*
dish of the day	今日の料理	*kyoh-no ryohri*
disinfectant	消毒剤	*shohdoku-zigh*
distance	距離	*kyori*
distilled water	蒸留水	*joh-ryoo-swee*
disturb	じゃまする	*jama suru*
disturbance	妨害	*boh-gigh*
dive	潜る	*moguru*

diving	スキンダイビング	*skin-dighbingu*
diving board	飛び込み台	*tobikomi-digh*
diving gear	スキンダイビング・セット	*skin-dighbingu-setto*
divorced	離婚した	*rikon shta*
Do-it-yourself store	日曜大工店	*nichiyoh-dighku-ten*
dizzy	めまい	*me-migh*
do	する	*suru*
doctor	医者	*isha*
dog	犬	*inu*
doll	人形	*ningyoh*
domestic	国内	*koku-nigh*
done (cooked)	よく料理した	*yoku ryohri shta*
door	戸／ドア	*to/doa*
double	ダブル	*daburu*
down	下	*shta*
draft (air)	すき間風	*skima-kazay*
dream (verb)	(…を) 夢に見る	*(... o) yumay-ni miru*
dress	ドレス	*dores*
dressing gown	部屋着	*heya-gi*
drink (medicine)	薬を飲む	*kusuri-o nomu*
drink (verb)	飲む	*nomu*
drinking water	飲料水	*Inryoh-swee*
drive	運転する	*unten suru*
driver	運転手	*untenshu*
driver's licence	運転免許	*unten menkyo*
druggist	薬局	*yakkyoku*
dry	かわいた	*kawa-ita*
dry (verb)	干す	*hosu*
dry clean	ドライクリーニング	*drigh-kreeningu*
dry cleaner's	洗濯屋／	*sentakuya/*
	クリーニング店	*kreeningu-ten*
during	…中	*... choo*
during (in the middle of)	…の間に	*... no igh-da-ni*
during the day	昼間	*hiruma*

E

ear	耳	*mimi*
ear, nose and throat specialist	耳鼻・咽喉科	*jibi-inkoh-ka*
earache	耳痛	*jitsoo*
eardrops	耳薬	*mimi-kusuri*
early	早い	*haya-i*
earrings	イヤリング	*iyaringu*
earth	土地	*to-chi*
earthenware	陶器	*toh-ki*
east	東	*higashi*
easy (simple)	簡単な／容易な	*kantan-na/yoh-i-na*
easy (to use)	便利な	*benri-na*
eat	食べる	*taberu*
eczema	湿疹	*shisshin*
eel	ウナギ	*unagi*
egg	卵	*tamago*
eggplant	ナス	*nasu*
electric	電気 (の)	*denki (no)*
electricity	電気	*denki*
elevator	エレベーター	*ere-baytah*
embassy	大使館	*tigh-shikan*

emergency brake	緊急ブレーキ	*kinkyoo brayki*
emergency exit	非常口	*hijoh-guchi*
emergency phone	非常電話	*hijoh denwa*
emery board	つめやすり	*tsumay-yasuri*
emperor	天皇	*ten-noh*
empty	からの	*kara-no*
engaged (on the phone)	話し中	*hanashi-choo*
engaged (to be married)	婚約した	*kon-yak-shta*
England	イギリス	*Igirisu*
English (language)	英語	*ay-go*
enjoy	楽しむ	*tano-shimu*
envelope	封筒	*footoh*
escort	コンパニオン	*kompanion*
evening	夕方	*yoo-gata*
evening wear	ディナースーツ／ イブニングドレス	*dinah soots (men)/ eebuningu dores (women)*
event	事件／できごと	*jiken/dekigoto*
everything	全部	*zembu*
everywhere	どこにも	*doko-nimo*
examine	探る	*saguru*
excavation	発掘	*hakkuts*
excellent	優れた	*sugureta*
exchange	交換する	*kohkan suru*
exchange office	為替両替所	*kawase-ryoh-gae-jo*
exchange rate	為替レート	*kawase-rayto*
excursion	遊覧	*yooran*
exhibition	展覧会	*tenran-kigh*
exit	出口	*deguchi*
expenses	費用／経費	*hiyoh/kayhi*
expensive	高い	*ta-kigh*
explain	説明する	*setsumay suru*
express	急行電車	*kyookoh densha*
external	外	*soto*
eye	目	*me*
eye drops	目薬	*me-gusuri*
eye shadow	アイシャドー	*igh-shadoh*
eye specialist	眼科医／目医者	*ganka-i/me-isha*
eyeliner	アイライナー	*igh-righnah*

F

face	顔	*kao*
factory	工場	*koh-joh*
fall (verb)	ころぶ	*korobu*
family	家族	*kazoku*
famous	有名な	*yoo-may-na*
far away	遠く	*tohku*
farm	農家	*nohka*
farmer	お百姓	*ohyakusho*
fashion	ファッション	*fashon*
fast	速い	*ha-yigh*
father (other's)	お父さま	*o-toh-sama*
father (own)	父	*chichi*
fault	誤り	*ayamari*
fax (verb)	ファックスを送る	*fakkusu-o okuru*
February	二月	*ni-gats*
feel	感じる	*kanjiru*

feel like	好む	konomu
fence	垣根	kaki-ne
ferry	渡し船／	watashi-bunay/
	フェリーボート	feree-bohto
fever	熱	netsu
fill	詰める	tsumeru
fill out	書き込む	kaki-komu
filling	詰め物	tsumemono
film (cinema)	映画	ayga
film (photo)	フィルム	firumu
filter	フィルター	firutah
filter cigarette	フィルター付き	firutah-tski tabako
	タバコ	
find	見つける	mitsu-keru
fine (money)	罰金	bakkin
finger	指	yubi
fire	火	hi
fire (on)	火事	kaji
fire dept.	消防	shoh-boh
fire escape	非常階段	hijoh kigh-dan
fire extinguisher	消火器	shoh-ka-ki
first (in line)	最初に	sigh-sho-ni
first (number one)	第一／一番	dai-ichi/ichiban
first aid	応急手当て	ohkyoo te-atay
first class	一等	ittoh
fish	魚	sakana
fish (verb)	釣をする	tsuri-o suru
fishing rod	釣竿	tsuri-zao
fitness club	フィットネスセンター	fitnes-sentah
fitness training	フィットネス	fitnes
fitting room	試着室	shichaku-shits
fix (puncture)	パンクしたタイヤを	panku shta tigh-ya-o
	直す	na-osu
flag	旗	hata
flash	フラッシュ	furash
flea market	蚤の市	nomi-no-ichi
flight	飛行	hikoh
flight number	便名	bin-may
flood	大水	ohmizu
floor	階	kigh
flounder	カレイ	karay
flour	粉	kona
flu	インフルエンザ	infruenza
fly (insect)	ハエ	ha-e
fly (verb)	飛ぶ	tobu
fog	霧	kiri
foggy (to be)	霧がかかる	kiri-nga kakaru
folkloristic	民族伝統の	minzoku dentoh-no
follow	従う	shita-ga-u
food (items)	食品	shokuhin
food (stuffs)	食料	shoku-ryoh
food poisoning	食中毒	shoku-choodoku
foot	足	ashi
forbidden	禁止	kinshi
forehead	額	sh-tigh
foreign	外国の	gigh-koku-no
forget	忘れる	wasureru

fork	フォーク	fohku
form	用紙	yohshi
forward (a letter)	転送する	ten-soh suru
fountain	噴水	fun-swee
frame	額縁	gaku-buchi
free (no charge)	無料	muryoh
free (unoccupied)	空いている	igh-tay iru
free time	暇	hima
freeze	凍る	kohru
French bread	フランスパン	furansu-pan
french fries	フライドポテト	frighdo-poteto
fresh	新鮮な	shinsen-na
Friday	金曜日	kin-yoh-bi
fried	焼いた	yigh-ta
fried egg	目玉焼き	medama-yaki
friend	友達	tomo-dachi
friendly	心からの／親切な	kokoro-kara-no/ shinsetu-na
frightened	恐れる	osoreru
fruit	フルーツ／果物	froots/kudamono
fruit juice	ジュース	joosu
frying pan	フライパン	furigh-pan
full (tank)	満タン	mantan
fun	楽しい	tano-shee

G

gallery	画廊	garoh
game	ゲーム	gaym
garage (car repair)	修理屋	shoori-ya
garbage bag	ごみ袋	gomi-bukuro
garden	庭	niwa
garden	庭	niwa
gas	ガソリン	gasorin
gas station	ガソリンスタンド	gasorin stando
gear	ギア	gee-a
gel (hair)	ジェル	jeru
get married	結婚する	kekkon suru
get off	下車する／降りる	gesha suru/oriru
gift	贈り物／ギフト	okuri-mono/gift
gilt	金メッキ	kin-mekki
ginger	ショウガ	shoh-ga
girl	女の子	onna-no ko
girlfriend	ガールフレンド	gahru-frendo
giro check	小切手	kogittay
given name	名前	na-migh
glass	ガラス	garas
glass (drinking)	グラス／コップ	guras/koppu
glasses	眼鏡	me-ganay
glasses (sun-)	サングラス	san-guras
glide	グライダーに乗る	gu-righdah-ni noru
glove	手袋	te-bukuro
glue	のり	nori
gnat (mosquito)	蚊	ka
go	行く	iku
go back	戻る	modoru
go out	外出する	gigh-shuts suru
gold	金	kin

Word list

15

golf course	ゴルフ場	gorufu-jo
good afternoon/day	こんにちは	kon-nichi-wa
good evening/night	こんばんは	komban-wa
good morning	おはようございます	ohayoh goza-imas
good night	おやすみなさい	oyasumi-na-sigh
good bye	さようなら	sayoh-nara
grade crossing	踏切	fumi-kiri
gram	グラム	gram
grandchild	孫	mago
grandfather (other's)	おじいさん	o-jee-san
grandfather (own)	祖父	sofu
grandmother (other's)	お婆さん	obahsan
grandmother (own)	祖母	sobo
grape juice	グレープ・ジュース	grayp joosu
grapefruit	グレープフルーツ	graypu-furoots
grapes	ブドウ	budoh
grave	墓	haka
gray	灰色の／ねずみ色の	high-iro-no/nezumi-iro-no
gray (hair)	白髪	haku-hats
greasy	脂の多い	abura-no oh-ee
green	緑の	midori-no
greet	挨拶する	igh-sats suru
grill	網焼きをする／グリルする	amiyaki-o suru/guriru suru
grilled	ローストした	rohst shta
grocer	食料品店	shokuryoh-hin-ten
ground	土地	tochi
group	グループ	guroop
guest house	民宿／ペンション	minshuku/penshon
guide (book)	案内書	annigh-sho
guide (person)	ガイド	gigh-do
guided tour	ガイド付きツアー	gigh-do tsuki tsu-ah
gynecologist	産婦人科	san-fujin-ka

H

hair	髪	kami
hairbrush	ヘアブラシ	hea-burashi
hairdresser	床屋／美容院	tokoya/biyoh-in
hairpins	ヘアピン	hea-pin
hairspray	ヘア・スプレー	hea-spray
half	半分	hambun
half full	…を半分	... o hambun
hammer	かなずち	kana-zuchi
hand	手	te
hand brake	ハンド・ブレーキ	hando-burayki
handbag	ハンドバッグ	hando-baggu
handkerchief	ハンカチ	hankachi
handmade	手作り	te-zukuri
happy	嬉しい	ure-shee
harbor	港	minato
hard	堅い	ka-tigh
hat	帽子	bohshi
hay fever	花粉症	kafun-shoh
head	頭	atama
headache	頭痛	zutsoo
health	健康	kenkoh

health food shop	自然食品店	shizen shoku-hin-ten
hear	聞く	kiku
hearing aid	補聴器	hochoh-ki
heart	心臓	shinzoh
heart patient	心臓病患者	shinzoh-byoh kanja
heat	熱さ	atsusa
heater	ヒーター	heetah
heavy	重い	omo-i
heel	かかと	kakato
hello	こんにちは	kon-nichi-wa
helmet	ヘルメット	herumetto
help	助け	tasukay
help	助ける／手伝う	tas-keru/tetsu-dau
helping (of food)	一人前	shtori-migh
herbal tea	ハーブティー	hahbu-tee
herbs (seasonings)	調味料	chohmi-ryoh
here	ここ	koko
herring	ニシン	nishin
high	高い	ta-kigh
high tide	満潮	manchoh
highchair	子供用椅子	kodomo-yoh isu
highway	高速道路	kosoku doro
hiking	ハイキング	high-kingu
hiking boots	登山靴	toh-zan-guts
hip	腰	koshi
hire	賃貸する／借りる	chin-tigh suru/kariru
hitchhike	ヒッチハイクをする	hitchi-high-ku-o suru
hobby	趣味	shumi
hold-up	強盗	gohtoh
holiday	休暇／休み	kyooka/yasumi
holiday (festival)	祭日	sigh-jits
holiday (public)	休日	kyoo-jits
holiday park	休暇村	kyoo-ka mura
holiday rental	別荘	bessoh
homesickness	ホームシック	hohm-shikku
honest	正直な	shoh-jiki-na
honey	蜂蜜	hachi-mitsu
horizontal	水平の	swee-hay-no
horrible	大変	tigh-hen
horse	馬	uma
hospital	病院	byoh-in
hospitality	もてなし／接待	mote-nashi/set-tigh
hot	熱い／暑い	atsu-i
hot (bitter, sharp)	辛い	ka-righ
hot chocolate	ホットチョコレート	hotto-choko-rehto
hot spring	温泉	onsen
hotel	ホテル	hoteru
hot-water bottle	湯たんぽ	yoo-tampo
hour	時間	jikan
house	家／うち	ie/uchi
household items	家庭用品	katay yoh-hin
houses of parliament	国会議事堂	kok-kigh giji-doh
housewife	主婦	shufu
how far?	どのくらい（遠い）	dono gurigh (toh-i)
how long?	どのくらい（長い）	dono gurigh (na-gigh)

how much?	いくら	*ikura*
how?	どう	*doh*
hungry (to be)	空腹だ	*koofuku-da*
hurry	急速	*kyoosoku*
husband (other's)	ご主人	*goshujin*
husband (own)	夫/主人	*otto/shujin*
hut	小屋	*koya*

I

ice cubes	氷	*kohri*
ice skate	スケートをする	*skehto-o suru*
ice cream	アイスクリーム	*ighs-kreem*
idea	考え	*kan-ga-e*
identification (card)	身分証明書	*mibun shoh-may-sho*
identify	身分を証明する	*mibun-o shoh-may suru*
ignition key	始動キー	*shidoh kee*
ill	病気	*byoh-ki*
illness	病気	*byoh-ki*
imagine	想像する	*sohzoh suru*
immediately	すぐに	*sugu-ni*
import duty	輸入税	*yunyoo-zay*
impossible	無理な/不可能な	*muri-na/fukanoh-na*
in	…の中に	*....no naka-ni*
in the evening	夕方	*yoogata*
in the morning	午前	*gozen*
included	…を含めて	*.... o fukumete*
included	含めた	*fukumeta*
indicate	示す	*shi-mes*
indicator	方向指示器	*hohkoh-shijiki*
industrial art	工芸	*koh-gay*
inexpensive	安い	*yasu-i*
infection	伝染	*densen*
(viral, bacterial)	(ビールスの、 バクテリアの)	*(beerus-no, bakuteria-no)*
inflammation	炎症	*enshoh*
information	情報	*joh-hoh*
information (guide)	案内	*an-nigh*
information (material)	資料	*shiryoh*
information office	案内所	*an-nigh-sho*
injection	注射	*choosha*
injured	負傷した	*f-shoh shta*
inner tube	チューブ	*choob*
innocent	無罪な	*mu-zigh-na*
insect	こん虫	*konchoo*
insect bite	虫さされ	*mushi-sasaray*
insect repellent	虫除けクリーム	*mushi-yokay kreem*
inside	中に/内に	*naka-ni/uchi-ni*
insole	靴の内底	*kutsu-no nigh-tay*
instructions	使用法	*shiyoh-hoh*
insurance	保険	*hoken*
intermission	休憩	*kyookay*
international	国際の	*koku-sigh-no*
interpreter	通訳者	*tsooyakusha*
intersection	交差点	*kohsaten*
introduce (oneself)	紹介する	*shoh-kigh suru*
invite	招待する	*shoh-tigh suru*

iodine	赤チン	*aka-chin*
Ireland	アイルランド	*igh-ru-rando*
iron (clothes)	アイロン	*igh-ron*
iron (metal)	鉄	*tetsu*
iron (verb)	アイロンをかける	*igh-ron-o kakeru*
ironing board	アイロン台	*igh-ron-digh*
island	島	*shima*
itch	かゆい	*kayui*

J

jack	ジャッキ	*jakki*
jacket	ジャケット	*jaketto*
jam	ジャム	*jamu*
January	一月	*ichi-gats*
Japanese-style bar	居酒屋	*izakaya*
jaw	顎	*ago*
jellyfish	クラゲ	*kuragay*
jeweler	貴金属店／宝石店	*kikinzoku-ten/ hohseki-ten*
jewelery	装身具	*soh-shin-gu*
jog	ジョギング	*joggingu*
joke	冗談	*joh-dan*
juice	ジュース	*joosu*
July	七月	*shich-gats*
June	六月	*roku-gats*

K

key	キー／鍵	*kee/kagi*
kilo	キロ（グラム）	*kiro(gram)*
kilometer	キロ（メートル）	*kito(mehtoru)*
kiss	キス	*kisu*
kiss (verb)	キスする	*kisu suru*
kitchen	台所	*digh-dokoro*
knee	膝	*hiza*
knee socks	ニー・ソックス／ ハイソックス	*nee-sokkusu/high- sokkusu*
knife	ナイフ	*nighfu*
knit	編む	*amu*
know	知る	*shiru*

L

lace	レース	*raysu*
lace (shoes)	靴ひも	*kutsu-himo*
ladies' room	婦人用トイレ	*fujinyoh toy-ray*
lake	湖	*mizu-umi*
lamp	ランプ	*ramp*
land (ground)	土地	*tochi*
land (verb)	着陸する	*chaku-riku suru*
lane (of traffic)	車線	*shasen*
language	言葉／言語	*kotoba/gengo*
large	大きい	*ohkee*
last	最後／最終	*sigh-go/sigh-shoo*
last night	昨晩	*sakuban*
late	遅い	*oso-i*
later	後程	*nochi hodo*
laugh	笑う	*wara-u*
launderette	コインランドリー	*koyn randoree*

Word list

15

laundry soap	洗剤	sen-zigh
law	法律	hohrits
lawyer	弁護士	ben-goshi
laxative	下剤	ge-zigh
leak (air)	パンク	panku
leather	皮	kawa
leather goods	皮製品	kawa-say-hin
leave	出発する	shuppats suru
leek	長ネギ	naga-negi
left	左	hidari
left (to turn)	左に曲がる	hidari-ni magaru
leg	足	ashi
lemon	レモン	remon
lend	…に貸す	... ni kasu
lens	レンズ	renz
less	少なく	sku-naku
lesson	レッスン	ressun
letter	手紙	tegami
lettuce	レタス	retasu
library	図書館	toshokan
lie	うそ	uso
lie (down)	横になっている	yoko-ni nattay iru
lie (to tell a)	うそをつく	uso-o tsku
lift (hitchhike)	ヒッチハイク	hitchi-high-ku
lift (ski)	リフト	rifto
light	ライト	right-to
light (not dark)	明るい	aka-rui
light (not heavy)	軽い	ka-rui
lighter	ライター	right-tah
lighthouse	灯台	toh-digh
lightning	稲妻／稲光／かみなり	inazuma/ina-bikari/ kaminari
like (verb)	好む／好き	konomu/ski
line	線	sen
linen	麻／リネン	asa/rinen
lipstick	口紅	kuchi-beni
liquor store	酒屋	saka-ya
liqueur	リキュール	rikyooru
listen	聞く	kiku
literature	文学	bun-gaku
liter	リットル	rittoru
little (amount)	少ない	sku-nigh
live	住む	sumu
lobster	伊勢えび	isay-ebi
lock	鍵／錠前	kagi/johma-e
long	長い	na-gigh
long distance call	長距離電話	choh-kyori denwa
look	見る	miru
look for	捜す	sagasu
look up	調べる	shiraberu
lose (verb)	失う／なくす	ushina-u/nakusu
loss	損失	sonshits
lost	失った	ushinatta
lost (to be)	道に迷う	michi-ni mayo-u
lost item	遺失物	ish-ts-buts
lost and found office	遺失物取扱所	ish-ts-buts tori-atsu- kigh-jo

lotion	ローション	rohshon
loud (voice)	大声で	ohgo-e-de
love	愛／愛情	igh/aigh-joh
love (verb)	愛する	igh-suru
love with (to be in)	愛している	igh-shtay iru
low	低い	hiku-i
low tide	干潮／引き潮	kanchoh/hiki-shio
LPG	プロパン	propan
luck	幸運	koh-un
luggage	荷物	nimots
luggage locker	コイン・ロッカー	koyn rokkah
lumps (sugar)	角砂糖	kaku-zatoh
lunch	昼食	choo-shoku
lunch room (cafe)	コーヒーショップ／	koh-hee-shoppu/
	喫茶店	kissaten
lungs	肺	high

M

macaroni	マカロニ	makaroni
madam	…さん	...-san
magazine	雑誌	zasshi
mail	郵便	yoobin
mailman	郵便屋さん	yoobin-ya-san
main post office	郵便局本局／	yoobin-kyoku hon-
	中央郵便局	kyoku /choo-oh
		yoobin-kyoku
main road	大通り	ohdohri
make an appointment	約束する	yak-soku suru
make love	セックスする	sekkusu suru
makeshift	一時的な	ichiji-teki-na
man	男	otoko
manager (caretaker)	管理人	kanri-nin
mandarin (fruit)	ミカン	mikan
manicure	マニキュア	manikyua
many	たくさん	tak-san
map	地図	chizu
marble	大理石	digh-ri-seki
March	三月	san-gats
margarine	マーガリン	mahgarin
marina	ヨット用ドック／	yotto-yoh
	マリーナ	dokku/mareena
market	市場／マーケット	ichiba/mahketto
marriage	結婚	kekkon
married	結婚した	kekkon shta
Mass	ミサ	misa
massage	マッサージ	massahji
match	試合	shi-igh
matches	マッチ	matchi
matte (photo)	光沢のない	kohtaku-no nigh
May	五月	go-gats
maybe	多分	tabun
mayonnaise	マヨネーズ	mayonehzu
mayor	市長	shi-choh
meal	食事	shokuji
mean (verb)	意味する	imi suru
meat	肉	niku
medication	薬／薬品	kusuri/yakuhin

medicine	薬品／薬	*yakuhin/kusuri*
medicine for diarrhea	下痢止め	*geri-dome*
meet	…に会う	*... ni au*
melon	メロン	*meron*
melon (water)	西瓜	*sweeka*
membership (card)	会員証	*kigh-in-shoh*
menstruate	月経がある	*gekkay-ga-aru*
menstruation	生理／メンス	*sayri/mensu*
menu	メニュー／献立	*menyoo/kondatay*
menu of the day	本日のメニュー	*honjitsu no menyoo*
message	伝言	*dengon*
metal	金属	*kinzoku*
meter (in taxi)	メーター	*mehtah*
meter (100 cm)	メートル	*mehtoru*
migraine	偏頭痛	*henzutsoo*
mild (tobacco)	軽い	*karui*
milk	牛乳／ミルク	*gyoo-nyoo/miruku*
millimeter	ミリ	*miri*
	（メートル）	*(mehtoru)*
mineral water	ミネラルウォーター	*mineraru-wohtah*
minute	分	*fun*
mirror	鏡	*kagami*
miss (a person)	寂しくなる	*sabishku-naru*
missing (to be)	不足する	*fusoku suru*
missing person	迷子	*migh-go*
mistake	間違い	*machi-gigh*
mistaken (to be)	間違える	*machi-ga-eru*
misunderstanding	誤解	*go-kigh*
mixture (medicine)	飲み薬	*nomi-gusuri*
mocha	モカ	*moka*
modern art	現代の芸術	*gen-digh-no gay-juts*
molar	奥歯	*okuba*
moment	瞬間	*shunkan*
moment (just a)	ちょっと	*chotto*
monastery	修道院	*shoodoh-in*
Monday	月曜日	*gets-yohbi*
money	お金	*o-kanay*
month	月	*tski*
moped	モペット	*mopetto*
motel	モーテル	*mohteru*
mother (other's)	お母さま	*o-kah-sama*
mother (own)	母	*haha*
motor cross	モトクロス	*moto-kurosu*
motorbike	バイク	*bighk*
motorboat	モーターボート	*mohtah-bohto*
mountain	山	*yama*
mountain hut	山小屋	*yama-goya*
mouse	ネズミ	*nezumi*
mouth	口	*kuchi*
much	たくさん	*tak-san*
muscle	筋	*suji*
muscle spasms	筋肉けいれん	*kinniku kayren*
museum	美術館／博物館	*bijutsu-kan/*
		hakubutsu-kan
mushrooms	キノコ	*kinoko*
music	音楽	*on-gaku*
musical	ミュージカル	*myoojikaru*

mussels	イガイ／ムール貝	i-gigh/mooru-gigh
mustard	からし／マスタード	karashi/mastahdo

N

nail	釘	kugi
nail (finger)	つめ	tsumay
nail scissors	つめ切り	tsumay-kiri
naked	裸／ヌード	hadaka/noodo
nationality	国籍	koku-seki
natural	自然の	shizen-no
nature	自然	shizen
naturism	裸体主義	ra-tigh-shugi
nauseous	気分が悪い	kibun-nga waru-i
near	…の近くに	... no chikaku-ni
nearby	ごく近く	goku-chikaku
necessary	…が必要	... nga hitsuyoh
neck	首	kubi
necklace	ネックレス	nekkuraysu
needle	針	hari
negative (photo)	ネガ	nega
neighbors	隣の人	tonari-no shto
nephew	甥	oi
never	全然…ない／	zenzen ... nigh/
	全く…ない	mattaku ... nigh
new	新しい	atara-shee
news	ニュース	nyoos
news stand	キオスク／売店	kiosk/bigh-ten
newspaper	新聞	shimbun
next	次の	tsugi-no
next to	…のそばに	... no soba-ni
nice	楽しい／快適な	tanoshee/kigh-teki-na
nice (friendly)	親切	shin-sets
nice (happy)	うれしい	ureshee
nice (person)	かわいい／よい	kawa-ee/yoi
nice (taste)	おいしい	oi-shee
niece	姪	may
night	夜	yoru
night duty	夜勤	yakin
nightclub	ナイト・クラブ	nighto-kurabu
nipple (bottle)	乳首	chi-kubi
no	いいえ	ii-ye
no passing	追い越し禁止	oi-koshi kinshi
noise	うるさい／騒音	uru-sigh/soh-on
nonstop (plane)	直行	chokkoh
no one	だれも…ない	daray-mo ... nigh
normal	普通	futsoo
north	北	kita
nose	鼻	hana
nose drops	鼻薬	hana-gusuri
note pad	メモ帳	memo-cho
notepaper	便箋	binsen
nothing	何も…ない	nani-mo ... nigh
November	十一月	joo-ichi-gats
nowhere	どこにも…ない	doko-nimo ... nigh
nude beach	ヌーディスト・ビーチ	noodisto beech
number	番号	ban-go

number plate	ナンバー・プレート	nanbah-purayto
nurse	看護婦	kangofu
nutmeg	ナツメッグ	natsumeggu
nuts	ナッツ／おつまみ	nattsu/otsumami

O

October	十月	joo-gats
off (gone bad)	くさった	kusatta
offer	申し出る	mohshi-deru
office	事務所／オフィス	jimusho/ofiss
oil	油／オイル	abura/oiru
oil level	オイルの量	oiru-no ryoh
ointment	軟膏	nankoh
ointment for burns	火傷の軟膏	yakedo-no nanko
okay	OK	OK
old (thing/person)	古い／年とった	furui/toshi-totta
olive oil	オリーブ油	oreebu-yoo
olives	オリーブ	oreebu
omelette	オムレツ	omurets
on	…の上に	... no ue-ni
on board (to go)	乗船する	johsen suru
on the right	右の方に	migi-no hoh-ni
on the way	途中で	tochoo-de
oncoming car	対向車	tigh-koh-sha
one-way traffic	一方通行	ippoh tsookoh
onion	玉ねぎ	tama-negi
open (to be)	開いている	ightay-iru
open (verb)	開ける	akeru
opera	オペラ	opera
operate (surgeon)	手術する	shujuts suru
operator (telephone)	交換手	kohkanshu
opposite	向こう側	mukoh-gawa
optician	眼鏡屋	megane-ya
orange	オレンジ	orenji
orange (color)	オレンジ色	orenji-iro
orange juice	オレンジ・ジュース	orenji-joosu
order	注文	choomon
order (tidy)	片づいた	kata-zuita
order (verb)	注文する	choomon suru
other	他の	hoka-no
other side	向こう側	mukoh-gawa
outside	外	soto
overpass	高架橋	kohka-kyoh
over there	あそこ	asoko
overtake	追い越す	oi-kosu
oysters	カキ	kaki

P

packed lunch	弁当	bentoh
page	ページ	payji
pain	痛み	itami
painkiller	痛み止め／鎮痛剤	itami-domay/ chin-tsoo-zigh
paint	ペンキ	penki
painting	絵画	kigh-ga
pajamas	パジャマ	pajyama
palace	宮殿／皇居	kyooden/kohkyo

pan	鍋	*nabay*
pancake	パンケーキ	*pan-kehki*
pancake (Japanese style)	ホットケーキ	*hotto-kehki*
pane	窓ガラス	*mado-garas*
pants	ズボン／スラックス	*zubon/surakks*
paper	紙	*kami*
paprika	ピーマン	*peeman*
paraffin oil	パラフィン油／灯油	*parafin-yoo/tohyoo*
parasol	日傘	*higasa*
parcel	小包み	*ko-zutsu-mi*
pardon	すみません	*sumimasen*
parents (other's)	ご両親	*go-ryohshin*
parents (own)	両親	*ryohshin*
park	公園	*koh-en*
park (verb)	駐車する	*choosha suru*
parking garage	駐車場	*choosha-jo*
parking space (meter)	駐車メーター	*choosha mehtah*
parsley	パセリ	*paseri*
part (car-)	部品	*buhin*
partner	恋人	*koi-bito*
party	パーティー	*pahtay*
passable (road)	通行出来る	*tsoo-koh dekiru*
passenger	旅客	*ryokyaku*
passport	パスポート	*pasupohto*
passport photo	証明写真	*shoh-may shashin*
patient	病人	*byohnin*
pavement	歩道	*hodoh*
pay	払う	*hara-u*
pay the bill	勘定を払う	*kanjoh-o hara-u*
peach	桃	*momo*
peanuts	ピーナッツ	*peenattsu*
pear	梨	*nashi*
peas	グリーンピース	*gureenpeesu*
pedal	ペダル	*pedaru*
pedestrian crossing	横断歩道	*ohdan-hodoh*
pedicure	ペディキュア	*pedikyua*
pedometer	万歩計	*mampo-kay*
pen	ペン	*pen*
pencil	鉛筆	*empits*
penis	ペニス	*penis*
pepper	胡椒	*koshoh*
performance	上演	*joh-en*
perfume	香水	*kohswe*
perm (hair)	パーマ（ネント）	*pahma (nento)*
perm (verb)	パーマをかける	*pahma-o kakeru*
permit	許可書	*kyoka-sho*
person	…人	*...-nin*
personal	個人的	*kojinteki*
pets	ペット	*petto*
pharmacy	薬局	*yak-kyok*
phone (tele-)	電話	*denwa*
phone (verb)	電話をかける	*denwa-o kakeru*
phone booth	電話ボックス	*denwa bokkusu*
phone directory	電話帳	*denwa-choh*
phone number	電話番号	*denwa-ban-goh*
photo	写真	*shashin*
photocopier	コピーマシン	*kopee-mashin*

photocopy	コピー	*kopee*
photocopy (verb)	コピーする	*kopee suru*
pick up (come to)	取りに来る	*tori-ni kuru*
pick up (go to)	取って来る	*tottay kuru*
picnic	ピクニック	*pikunikku*
pier	埠頭	*f-toh*
pigeon	ハト	*hato*
pill (contraceptive)	避妊薬／ピル	*hi-nin-yaku/piru*
pillow	枕	*makura*
pillowcase	枕カバー	*makura-kabah*
pin	ピン／留め針	*pin/tomebari*
pineapple	パイナップル	*pighn-appuru*
pipe	パイプ	*pighpu*
pipe tobacco	パイプ用たばこ	*pighpu-yoh tabako*
pity	残念	*zannen*
place of interest	みどころ／観光地	*midokoro/kankoh-chi*
plan	計画	*kay-kaku*
plant	植物	*shokubuts*
plastic	プラスチック	*puraschik*
plastic bag	ビニール袋	*bineeru-bukuro*
plate	皿	*sara*
platform	（プラット）ホーム	*(puratto) hohmu*
play	劇	*geki*
play (verb)	遊ぶ	*asobu*
play golf	ゴルフをする	*gorufu-o suru*
play sports	スポーツをする	*spohts-o suru*
play tennis	テニスをする	*tenisu-o suru*
playground	遊園地	*yoo-en-chi*
playing cards	トランプ	*torampu*
pleasant	気持ちのよい	*kimochi-no-yoi*
please	お願いします	*o-ne-gigh-shimas*
pleasure	楽しみ	*tano-shimi*
plum	梅	*umay*
pocketknife	ポケットナイフ	*poketto-nighfu*
point	指さす	*yubi sasu*
poison	毒	*doku*
police	警察	*kay-sats*
police station	警察署／交番	*kay-satsu-sho/kohban*
policeman	警察官／おまわりさん	*kaysats-kan/omawari-san*
pond	池	*ikay*
pony	ポニー馬	*ponee-uma*
population	人口	*jinkoh*
pork	豚肉	*buta-niku*
port	ポートワイン	*pohto-wighn*
porter	赤帽	*akaboh*
porter (concierge)	門番／守衛	*momban/shu-ay*
post (zip) code	郵便番号	*yoobin ban-go*
post office	郵便局	*yoobin-kyoku*
postage	郵便料金	*yoobin ryohkin*
postbox	ポスト／郵便箱	*posto /yoobin bako*
postcard	葉書／絵葉書	*hagaki/e-hagaki*
postman	郵便屋さん	*yoobin-ya-san*
potato	ジャガイモ	*jaga-imo*
potato chips	ポテトチップ	*poteto-chippu*
poultry	家禽	*kakin*
powdered milk	粉ミルク	*kona-miruku*
power outlet	コンセント	*konsento*

prawns	小エビ	ko-ebi
precious	貴重	kichoh
prefer	…方が好きだ	... hoh-nga ski da
preference	好み	konomi
pregnant	妊娠	nin-shin
prescription	処方	shohoh
present (not absent)	出席	shus-seki
present (gift)	プレゼント	purezento
press	押す	osu
pressure	圧力	atsu-ryoku
price	値段	nedan
price list	値段表	nedan-hyoh
print	プリント	printo
print (verb)	プリントする	printo suru
probably	多分	tabun
problem	問題	mon-digh
profession	職業	shoku-gyoh
program	プログラム	program
pronounce	発音する	hatsuon suru
propane camping gas	プロパン・ガス	propan-gas
pudding (caramel)	プディング／プリン	pudingu/purin
pull	引く	hiku
pull a muscle	筋肉を痛める	kin-niku-o itameru
pulse	脈	myaku
pure	純粋な	junswee-na
purple	紫色	murasaki-iro
purse	ハンドバッグ	hando-baggu
purse (money)	サイフ	sigh-f
push	押す	osu
puzzle	なぞ／パズル	nazo/pazuru

Q

quarter	四分の一	yombun-no ichi
quarter of an hour	十五分	joo-gofun
queen	女王	jo-oh
question	質問	shitsumon
quick	速く	hayaku
quiet	静かな	shizuka-na

R

radio	ラジオ	rajio
railways	鉄道	tetsudoh
rain	雨	amay
rain (verb)	雨が降る	amay-ga furu
raincoat	レインコート	rayn-kohto
raisins	干ぶどう	hoshi-budoh
rape	強姦	gohkan
rapids	急流	kyooryoo
raspberries	木イチゴ	ki-ichigo
raw	生の	nama-no
raw ham	生ハム	nama-hamu
raw vegetables	生の野菜	nama-no ya-sigh
razor blades	かみそり	kamisori
read	読む	yomu
ready	用意の出来た	yoh-i-no dekita
really	ほんとうに	hontoh-ni
receipt	領収書／受取書	ryoh-shuh-sho/uketorisho

Word list

recipe	料理法	*ryohri-hoh*
reclining chair	リクライニング・チェア	*rikrighning chea*
recommend	推薦する	*sweesen suru*
rectangle	長方形	*choh-hoh-kay*
red	赤い	*a-kigh*
red wine	赤ワイン	*aka-wighn*
reduction	減少	*genshoh*
refrigerator	冷蔵庫	*rayzoh-ko*
regards	…によろしく	*... ni yoroshku*
region	地方	*chihoh*
registered	書留	*kaki-tomay*
relatives	家族	*kazoku*
reliable	確かな	*tash-ka-na*
religion	宗教	*shoo-kyoh*
rent out	賃貸する	*chin-tigh suru*
repair	修理をする	*shoori-o suru*
repairs	修理	*shoori*
repeat	繰り返す	*kuri-ka-esu*
report (police)	調書	*choh-sho*
reserve	予約する	*yoyaku suru*
responsible	責任がある	*sekinin-ga aru*
rest	休憩する／休む	*kyookay suru/yasumu*
restaurant	レストラン	*resutoran*
result	結果	*kekka*
retired	退職した	*tigh-shoku shta*
return (ticket)	往復（切符）	*ohf-ku (kippu)*
reverse (vehicle)	バックする	*bakk suru*
rheumatism	リューマチ	*ryoomachi*
rice (cooked)	ごはん	*gohan*
rice (grain)	米	*komay*
ridiculous	ばかな／よしたまえ	*baka-na/yoshi-tama-e*
riding (horseback)	乗馬	*johba*
riding school	乗馬学校	*johba gakkoh*
right	右	*migi*
right of way	優先	*yoosen*
ripe	熟した	*juku shta*
risk	危険	*kiken*
river	川	*kawa*
road	道路	*dohro*
roadway	自動車道	*jidohsha-doh*
roasted	焼いた	*yigh-ta*
rock	岩	*iwa*
roll	ロールパン	*rohru-pan*
roof rack	ルーフ・ラック	*roof-rakku*
room	部屋	*he-ya*
room number	部屋番号	*he-ya ban-go*
room service	ルーム・サービス	*room sahbis*
rope	紐／ロープ	*himo/rohp*
rosé (wine)	ロゼ	*rozay*
rotary	ロータリー	*rohtaree*
route	道	*michi*
rowing boat	ボート	*bohto*
rubber	ゴム	*gomu*
rubber band	ゴム輪	*gomu-wa*
rude	失礼な	*shits-ray-na*
ruins	廃虚	*high-kyo*

run into	…に出会う	... ni de-au
running shoes	スポーツ・シューズ	spohts-shooz

S

sad	悲しい	kana-shee
safe (adj.)	安全な	anzen-na
safe	金庫	kinko
safety pin	安全ピン	anzen-pin
sail (verb)	ヨットを走らせる	yotto-o hashiraseru
sailing boat	ヨット	yotto
salad	サラダ	sarada
salad oil	サラダ油	sarada-yoo
salami	サラミソーセージ	sarami sohsehji
sale	売り出し	uridashi
salt	塩	shio
same	同じ	onaji
sandy beach	砂浜	suna-hama
sanitary pad	生理用ナプキン	sayri-yoh napkin
sardines	イワシ	iwashi
satisfied	満足した	manzoku shta
Saturday	土曜日	do-yoh-bi
sauce	ソース	sohsu
sauna	サウナ	sauna
sausage	ソーセージ	sohsehji
say	言う	yoo
scarf	スカーフ／マフラー	skahf/mafurah
scenic walk	散歩道	sampo-michi
school	学校	gakkoh
scissors	はさみ	hasami
scooter	スクーター	skootah
Scotch tape	セロテープ	serotehpu
Scotland	スコットランド	Skottorando
scrambled eggs	煎り卵	iri-tamago
screw	ねじ	neji
screwdriver	ねじ回し／ドライバー	neji-mawashi/dorighbah
sculpture	彫刻	choh-kok
sea	海	umi
seasick	船酔い	funa-yoi
seat	座席	zaseki
second	秒	byoh
second (in line)	第二	digh-ni
second-hand	中古品	chooko-hin
sedative	鎮静剤	chinsay-zigh
see	見る	miru
see (go sightseeing)	観光に行く	kankoh-ni iku
self-timer	セルフ・タイマー	serufu-tighmah
send	送る	okuru
sentence	文章	bunshoh
September	九月	ku-gats
serious	深刻な	shinkoku-na
service	サービス	sahbis
serviette	ナプキン	napukin
set	セット	setto
sewing needs	裁縫道具	sigh-hoh dohgu
shade	陰	kagay
shallow	浅い	a-sigh
shammy (chamois)	セーム皮	sehmu-gawa

Word list

15

shampoo	シャンプー	shampoo
shark	サメ／フカ	samay/f-ka
shave	剃る	soru
shaver	シェーバー／電気かみそり	shaybah/denki kamisori
shaving brush	ひげ剃り用ブラシ	hige-sori-yoh burashi
shaving cream	シェービング・クリーム	shaybingu-kureemu
shaving soap	ひげ剃り用石けん	hige-sori-yoh sekken
sheet	シーツ	sheets
sherry	シェリー	she-ree
shirt	シャツ	shats
shoe	靴	ku-tsu
shoe polish	靴クリーム	kutsu-kureemu
shoe shop	靴屋	ku-tsu-ya
shoemaker	靴直し	kutsu-naoshi
shop	店	misay
shop (verb)	買い物をする	kigh-mono-o suru
shop assistant	販売員／店員	han-bigh-in/ten-in
shop window	ショーウィンドー	shoh-windoh
shopping center	ショッピングセンター	shoppingu-sentah
short	短い	miji-kigh
short circuit	ショート	shohto
shorts	半ズボン	han-zubon
shoulder	肩	kata
show	ショー／上演	shoh/joh-en
shower	シャワー	shawah
shutter	シャッター	shattah
sieve	ふるい	furui
sign (name)	署名する	shomay suru
sign (road)	交通標識	kohtsoo hyoh-shiki
signature	署名／サイン	sho-may/sign
silence	沈黙／静けさ	chinmoku/shizukesa
silver	銀	gin
silver-plated	銀メッキの	ginmekki-no
simple	単純な	tanjun-na
single	シングル	shinguru
single (one way)	片道	katamichi
single (unmarried)	独身の	dokushin-no
sir	…さん	...-san
sister (elder, other's)	お姉さん	o-nay-san
sister (elder, own))	姉	anay
sister (younger, other's)	妹さん	imohto-san
sister (younger, own)	妹	imohto
sit	座る	suwaru
size	サイズ	sighzu
ski	スキーする	skee suru
ski boots	スキー靴	skee-gutsu
ski goggles	スキー用ゴーグル	skee-yoh gohguru
ski instructor	スキー指導員	skee shidoh-in
ski lessons/class	スキーレッスン／教室	skee ressun/kyoh-shtsu
ski lift	スキーリフト	skee-rifuto
ski pants	スキーズボン／スキー用パンツ	skee-zubon/skee-yoh pants
ski pole	ストック	stokku
ski slope	ゲレンデ	gerenday

ski suit	スキースーツ	skee-soots
ski wax	スキー用ワックス	skee-yoh wakkusu
skin	肌	hada
skirt	スカート	sukahto
skis	スキー	skee
sleep	眠る	nemuru
sleeping car	寝台車	shin-digh-sha
sleeping pills	睡眠薬	sui-min-yaku
slide	スライド	su-righdo
slip	シミーズ／ペティコート	shimeez/petikohto
slow	ゆっくり	yukkuri
slow train	各駅列車	kaku-eki ressha
small	小さい	chee-sigh
small change	小銭	kozeni
smell	臭う	ni-ou
smoke	煙	kemuri
smoked	薫製した	kunsay shta
smoking	喫煙	kitsu-en
smoking compartment	喫煙車	kitsu-en-sha
snake	ヘビ	hebi
snorkel	スノーケル	snohkeru
snow	雪	yuki
snow (verb)	雪が降る	yuki-ga furu
snow chains	チェーン	chayn
soap	石けん	sekken
soap box	石けん箱	sekken-bako
soap powder	粉石けん	kona-sekken
soccer	サッカー	sakkah
soccer match	サッカー試合	sakkah-ji-igh
socket	コンセント	konsento
socks	靴下／ソックス	kutsu-shta/sokkusu
soft drink	ソフト・ドリンク	sofut-dorinku
sole (fish)	舌びらめ	shta-biramay
sole (shoe)	靴底	kutsu-soko
someone	誰か	daray-ka
sometimes	時々	toki-doki
somewhere	どこか	doko-ka
son (other's)	息子さん	mus-ko-san
son (own)	息子	mus-ko
soon	早く	hayaku
sorbet	シャーベット	shahbetto
sore	傷	kizu
sore throat	のどの痛み	nodo-no itami
sorry	すみません	sumimasen
soup	スープ	soop
sour	すっぱい	sup-pigh
sour cream	サワークリーム	sawah-kureemu
south	南	minami
souvenir	おみやげ／おみやげ品	omiyagay/omiyage-hin
soy sauce	醤油	shoh-yu
spaghetti	スパゲッティ	spagetti
spare	予備	yobi
spare parts	予備部品	yobi-buhin
spare tire	予備のタイヤ	yobi-no tigh-ya
spare wheel	予備の車輪	yobi-no sharin
speak	話す	hanasu

Word list

15

special	特別な	tokubets-na
specialist (doctor)	専門医	semmon-i
speciality (cooking)	特別料理	tokubets ryohri
speed limit	最高速度	sigh-koh sokudo
spell	つづる	tsuzuru
spicy	スパイシー	spighshee
splinter	とげ	togay
spoon	スプーン	spoon
sport	スポーツ	spohtsu
sports center	スポーツ・センター	spohts-sentah
spot (place)	場所	basho
sprain	くじく	kujiku
spring	春	haru
square (plaza)	広場	hiroba
square (shape)	正方形	sayhoh-kay
square meters	平方メートル	hayhoh mehtoru
squash	スカッシュをする	skahsh-o suru
stadium	スタジアム	stajiam
stain	しみ	shimi
stain remover	しみ取り	shimi-tori
stairs	階段	kigh-dan
stamp	切手	kittay
start	動き出させる	ugoki-dasaseru
station	駅	eki
statue	像	zoh
stay (in hotel)	宿泊する	shuku-haku suru
stay (remain)	滞在	tigh-zigh
steal	盗む	nusumu
steel	鋼鉄	kohtets
stench	臭いにおい	ku-sigh ni-oi
sting (noun)	虫さされ	mushi-sasaray
stitch (med.)	（傷を）縫い合わせる	(kizu-o) nui-awaseru
stitch (verb)	縫う	noo
stock (soup)	スープの素	soop-no moto
stockings	ストッキング	stokkingu
stomach	胃	i
stomach (abdominal region)	腹／腹部	hara/fukubu
stomach ache	腹痛	fuku-tsoo
stomach cramps	激しい腹痛	hageshee fuku-tsoo
stools	糞便	fumben
stop	止まる	tomaru
stop (bus)	停留所／停車場	tay-ryoo-jo/tay-sha-jo
stopover	途中下車	tochoo-gesha
storm	嵐	arashi
straight	真っ直ぐ	massugu
straight ahead	真っ直ぐに	massugu-ni
straw	ストロー	sutoroh
strawberries	イチゴ	ichigo
street	道	michi
street side	道端	michibata
strike	スト（ライキ）	suto (righki)
strong	強い	tsuyo-i
study	勉強する	benkyoh suru
stuffing	詰め物	ts-me-mono
subtitled	字幕付きで	jimaki-tski-de
subway	地下	chika

subway station	地下鉄の駅	*chikatetsu-no eki*
subway system	地下鉄	*chikatetu*
succeed	出来る	*dekiru*
sugar	砂糖	*satoh*
suit	スーツ	*soots*
suitcase	スーツケース	*soots-kays*
summer	夏	*nats*
sun	太陽	*tigh-yoh*
sun hat	日よけ帽	*hiyoke-boh*
sunbathe	日光浴	*nikkoh-yoku*
Sunday	日曜日	*nichi-yoh-bi*
sunglasses	サングラス	*san-guras*
sunrise	日の出	*hinoday*
sunset	日暮れ	*higuray*
sunstroke	日射病	*nissha-byoh*
suntan lotion	日焼け止めクリーム	*hiyakedome kureemu*
suntan oil	日焼けオイル	*hiyake-oiru*
supermarket	スーパー（マーケット）	*soopah (mahketto)*
surcharge	追加料金	*tsuika ryohkin*
surf	サーフィンをする	*sahfin-o suru*
surf board	サーフボード	*sahfu-bohdo*
surname	苗字	*myoh-ji*
surprise	驚き	*odoroki*
swallow	飲みこむ	*nomi-komu*
swamp	沼地	*numa-chi*
sweat	汗	*asay*
sweater	セーター	*sehtah*
sweet	甘い	*ama-i*
sweet (kind)	親切な	*shin-sets-na*
sweet corn	トウモロコシ	*toh-moro-koshi*
swim	泳ぐ	*oyogu*
swimming pool	プール	*pooru*
swimming trunks	水泳パンツ	*swee-ay pants*
swindle	詐欺	*sagi*
switch	スイッチ	*switchi*
synagogue	ユダヤ教の会堂	*yudayakyoh-no kigh-doh*
syrup	シロップ	*shiroppu*

T

table	テーブル	*tehburu*
table tennis	卓球／ピンポン	*takkyoo/pin-pon*
tablet	錠剤	*joh-zigh*
take (medicine)	服用する	*fukuyoh suru*
take (photograph)	（写真を）撮る	*(shashin-o) toru*
take (time)	時間がかかる	*jikan-nga kakaru*
talcum powder	タルカム・パウダー	*tarukamu paudah*
talk	話す	*hanasu*
tall	背が高い	*say-nga ta-kigh*
tampons	タンポン	*tampon*
tanned	日に焼けた	*hi-ni yaketa*
tap	蛇口	*jaguchi*
tap water	水道の水	*sweedoh-no mizu*
taste (verb)	試す	*tamesu*
taste	味	*aji*

Word list

15

tax free shop	免税店	*menzay-ten*
taxi	タクシー	*takshee*
taxi stand	タクシー乗り場	*takshee noriba*
tea	お茶	*ocha*
tea (black)	紅茶	*kohcha*
tea (green)	緑茶	*ryokucha*
tea ceremony	お茶会	*ocha-kigh*
teapot	急須／ティーポット	*kyoosu/tee-pott*
teaspoon	茶さじ／ティースプーン	*chasaji/tee-spoon*
telegram	電報	*dempoh*
telephoto lens	望遠レンズ	*boh-en renzu*
television	テレビ	*terebi*
telex	テレックス	*terekkusu*
temperature (body)	体温	*tigh-on*
temperature (heat)	温度	*ondo*
temperature (weather)	気温	*kion*
temporary filling	一時的な虫歯の詰め物	*ichiji-teki-na mushiba-no tsumemono*
tender	柔らかい	*yawara-kigh*
tennis ball	テニスボール	*tenisu-bohru*
tennis court	テニスコート	*tenisu-kohto*
tennis racket	テニスラケット	*tenisu-raketto*
tent	テント	*tento*
tent peg	ペグ	*pegu*
terrace	テラス	*terasu*
terribly	大変な	*tigh-hen-na*
thank	お礼を言う	*oray-o yoo*
thank you	ありがとうございます	*arigatoh go-zigh-mas*
thanks	ありがとう	*arigatoh*
thaw	溶ける	*tokeru*
the day after tomorrow	あさって	*asattay*
theatre	劇場	*gekijo*
theft	窃盗	*settoh*
there	そこ	*soko*
thermal bath	温泉	*onsen*
thermometer (body)	体温計	*tigh-onkay*
thermometer (weather)	温度計	*ondokay*
thick	太い	*f-toy*
thief	泥棒	*doroboh*
thigh	太腿	*fto-momo*
thin (not fat)	細い／痩せた	*hoso-i/yaseta*
thin (not thick)	薄い	*usu-i*
think	思う	*omo-u*
think (consider)	考える	*kanga-eru*
third ($\frac{1}{3}$)	三分の一	*sambun no ichi*
thirsty (to be)	のどが渇く	*nodo-ga kawaku*
this afternoon	今日の午後	*kyoh-no gogo*
this evening	今晩	*komban*
this morning	今日の午前	*kyoh-no gozen*
thread	糸	*ito*
throat	喉	*nodo*
throat lozenges	せき止めドロップ	*seki-domay doroppu*
throw up	吐く	*haku*
thunderstorm	雷雨	*righ-u*
Thursday	木曜日	*moku-yohbi*
ticket	切符	*kippu*

ticket office (travel)	みどりの窓口	midori-no mado-guchi
ticket (admission)	入場券	nyoo-joh-ken
ticket (travel)	切符	kippu
tickets (seat)	座席券	zaseki-ken
tidy	片付ける	kata-zukeru
tie	ネクタイ	neku-tigh
tights	パンスト	pan-sto
time	時間	jikan
times	回	kigh
timetable	時刻表	jikoku-hyoh
tin (canned)	缶詰め	kanzu-may
tip	チップ	chippu
tire	タイヤ	tigh-ya
tire pressure	タイヤ圧力	tigh-ya atsu-ryoku
tissues	ティッシューペーパー	tisshoo-pehpah
toast	トースト	tohsto
tobacco	たばこ	tabako
toboggan	そり	sori
today	今日	kyoh
toe	足の指	ashi-no yubi
together	一緒に	issho-ni
toilet	トイレ／お手洗い／便所	toiray/o-te-a-righ/benjo
toilet paper	トイレットペーパー	toiretto-pehpah
toilet seat	便座	benza
toiletries	化粧品	keshoh-hin
tomato	トマト	tomato
tomato puree	トマトピューレー	tomato-pyooray
tomato sauce	トマトケチャップ	tomato-kechappu
tomorrow	明日	ashta
tongue	舌	shta
tonic water	トニック	tonikku
tonight	今晩／今夜	komban/konya
tools	道具	doh-gu
tooth	歯	ha
toothache	歯痛	ha-ita
toothbrush	歯ブラシ	ha-burashi
toothpaste	歯磨	ha-migaki
toothpick	ようじ	yohji
top up	おかわり	okawari
total	全部	zen-bu
tough	固い	ka-tigh
tour	ツアー／周遊／旅行	tsu-ah/shoo-yoo/ryokoh
tour guide	案内者／ガイド	an-nigh-sha/gighdo
tourist class	二等	nitoh
Tourist Information office	観光案内所	kankoh an-nigh-sho
tow	牽引する	ken-in suru
tow cable	牽引ロープ	ken-in rohpu
towel	タオル／手拭い	ta-oru/te-nugui
tower	塔	toh
town	町	machi
town hall	市役所	shiyakusho
toys	おもちゃ	omocha
traffic	交通	kohtsoo
traffic light	信号	shingo
train	列車	ressha

train (electric)	電車	*densha*
train ticket	切符	*kippu*
train timetable	時刻表	*jikoku-hyoh*
translate	翻訳する	*hon-yaku suru*
travel	旅行する	*ryokoh suru*
travel agent	旅行代理店	*ryokoh-dighri-ten*
travel guide	旅行案内／案内書	*ryokoh an-nigh/ an-nigh-sho*
traveler	旅行者	*ryokohsha*
traveler's check	旅行用小切手	*ryokoh-yoh kogittay*
treatment	治療	*chi-ryoh*
triangle	三角	*sankaku*
trim	切りそろえる	*kiri-soro-eru*
trip	旅行	*ryokoh*
trip (sightseeing)	観光	*kankoh*
trip (walk)	散歩	*sampo*
trout	マス（鱒）	*masu*
truck	トラック	*trakku*
trustworthy	たよりになる	*tayori-ni naru*
try on	試着する	*shichaku suru*
tube	チューブ	*choob*
Tuesday	火曜日	*ka-yohbi*
tumble drier	乾燥機	*kansohki*
tuna	マグロ	*maguro*
tunnel	トンネル	*tonneru*
turn	回	*kigh*
TV	テレビ	*terebi*
TV guide	テレビガイド	*terebi gigh-do*
tweezers	ピンセット	*pinsetto*
typhoon	台風	*tigh-foo*

U

ugly	みにくい／美しくない	*minikui/utsu-kushiku-nigh*
umbrella	傘	*kasa*
under	…の下に	*... no shta-ni*
underpants	パンツ	*pants*
understand	分かる／理解する	*wakaru/ri-kigh suru*
underwear	下着	*shta-gi*
undress	服を脱ぐ	*fuku-o nugu*
unemployed	失業	*shits-gyoh*
uneven (ground)	でこぼこの	*dekoboko-no*
university	大学	*digh-gaku*
unleaded	無鉛／ レギュラーガソリン	*mu-en/reguyrah-gasorin*
up	上	*ue*
urgent	非常／緊急	*hijoh/kinkyoo*
urgently	早急に	*sohkyoo-ni*
urine	小便／おしっこ	*shohben/oshikko*
usually	たいてい	*tigh-tay*

V

vacate	立ち退く	*tachi-noku*
vaccinate	予防接種	*yoboh sesshu*
vagina	膣	*chitsu*
valid	価値のある	*kachi-no aru*
valley	谷	*tani*

valuable	高価な	*kohka-na*
van	中型ヴァン／ミニバス	*choogata-van/minibas*
vanilla	バニラ	*banira*
vase	花瓶	*kabin*
vaseline	ワセリン	*waserin*
veal	小牛の肉	*ko-ushi-no niku*
vegetable soup	野菜スープ	*ya-sigh soop*
vegetables	野菜	*ya-sigh*
vegetarian	ベジタリアン／菜食家	*bejitarian/sigh-shokka*
vein	静脈	*joh-myaku*
vending machine	自動販売機	*jidoh ham-bigh-ki*
venereal disease	性病	*say-byoh*
via	経由	*kay-yoo*
video camera	ビデオ・カメラ	*bideo-kamera*
video recorder	ビデオレコーダー	*bideo-rekohdah*
video tape	ビデオテープ	*bideo-tehpu*
view	眺め	*nagamay*
village	村	*mura*
visa	ビザ	*biza*
visit	訪問する	*hohmon suru*
visiting card	名刺	*mayshi*
visiting time	面会時間	*menkigh jikan*
vitamin tablets	ビタミン剤	*bitamin-zigh*
vitamins	ビタミン	*bitamin*
volcano	火山	*kazan*
volleyball	バレーボール	*baray-bohru*
vomit	吐く／戻す	*haku/modosu*

W

wait	待つ	*matsu*
waiter	ウェーター	*waytah*
waiting room	待合室	*machi-a-i-shitsu*
waitress	ウェイトレス	*waytresu*
wake up	起きる	*okiru*
Wales	ウェールズ	*wayruzu*
walk (noun)	散歩	*sampo*
walk (verb)	散歩する／歩く	*sampo suru/aruku*
wallet	財布	*sighfu*
warm	温かい	*atatakigh*
warn	注意する	*choo-i suru*
warning	注意	*choo-i*
wash	洗う	*ara-u*
washing	洗濯物	*sentaku-mono*
washing line	物干しロープ	*mono-hoshi rohp*
washing machine	洗濯機	*sentakki*
wasp	スズメバチ	*suzume-bachi*
watch	腕時計	*uday-do-kay*
water	水	*mizu*
water ski	水上スキーをする	*sweejoh skee-o suru*
watermill	水車	*sweesha*
waterproof	防水	*bohswee*
wave-pool	人工波プール／波のあるプール	*jinkoh-ha pooru/nami-no aru pooru*
way (direction)	方面	*hohmen*
way (method)	手段／方法	*shudan/hoh-hoh*
we	私達	*watash-tachi*
weak	弱い	*yowa-i*

Word list

15

weather	天気	*tenki*
weather forecast	天気予報	*tenki yo-hoh*
wedding	結婚式	*kekkon-shki*
Wednesday	水曜日	*swee-yoh-bi*
week	週	*shoo*
weekend	週末	*shoo-mats*
weekly ticket	一週間の定期券	*isshookan-no tayki-ken*
welcome	いらっしゃい	*irassha-i*
well (good)	いい／良い	*ee/yoi*
well (water)	井戸	*ido*
west	西	*nishi*
wet	濡れた	*nureta*
wetsuit	ウェット・スーツ	*wetto-soots*
what?	何	*nani*
wheel	車輪	*sharin*
wheelchair	車いす	*kuruma-isu*
when?	いつ	*itsu*
where?	どこ	*doko*
which?	どちら	*dochira*
whipped cream	ホイップクリーム	*hoippu-kreem*
white	白い	*shiro-i*
who?	誰	*daray*
why?	なぜ	*nazay*
wide-angle lens	広角レンズ	*kohkaku renzu*
widow	未亡人	*mibohjin*
widower	男やもめ	*otoko-yamomay*
wife (other's)	奥さま	*okusama*
wife (own)	妻	*tsuma*
wind	風	*kazay*
windbreak	風よけ	*kazay-yokay*
windmill	風車	*foosha*
window	窓	*mado*
window (of ticket office)	窓口	*mado-guchi*
windshield wiper	ワイパー	*wigh-pah*
wine	ワイン	*wign*
wine list	ワインのメニュー	*wign-no menyoo*
wine shop	酒屋	*saka-ya*
winter	冬	*fuyu*
witness	証人	*shoh-nin*
woman	女	*onna*
wonderful (taste)	おいしい	*oy-shee*
wood	木	*ki*
wool (for knitting)	毛糸	*kay-to*
word	言葉	*kotoba*
work	仕事	*shi-goto*
working day (weekday)	平日	*hay-jits*
worn	古くなった	*furuku-natta*
worried	心配な	*shimpigh-na*
wound	傷	*kizu*
wrap	包む	*tsutsumu*
wrench	スパナー	*spanah*
wrist	手首	*tekubi*
write	書く	*kaku*
write down	書く	*kaku*
writing pad	便箋	*binsen*
writing paper	便箋	*binsen*

Word list

15

wrong	間違った	*machi-gatta*

Y

yacht	ヨット	*yotto*
year	年	*toshi/nen*
yellow	黄色い	*kee-roy*
yes	はい	*high*
yes, please	はい、いただきます／ お願いします	*high, itadaki-mas/* *onegigh-shimas*
yesterday	昨日	*kinoh*
yogurt	ヨーグルト	*yohguruto*
you	あなた	*anata*
you too	あなたも	*anata-mo*
youth hostel	ユースホステル	*yoos-hosteru*

Z

zip	ファスナー／ジッパー	*fasunah/jippah*
zoo	動物園	*doh-butsu-en*
zucchini	ズッキーニ	*zukkeenee*

Word list

Basic grammar

1 Sentence construction

The greatest difference between Japanese and English sentences is the position of the verb. In Japanese the verb always comes last, giving the basic structure as subject-object-verb:

sensei wa *michi* o **oshiemashita**   The teacher **showed** me the *way*

2 Parts of speech

Nouns Japanese nouns have no articles and no plural forms. **Zasshi** (magazine), for example, could mean a/the magazine, magazines, or the/some magazines. This might sound potentially confusing to English speakers who expect the clear distinctions that articles and plurals give. In actuality, though, very little confusion exists, because Japanese has ways of indicating number when it is necessary (see chapter 1).

Pronouns Japanese uses pronouns far less than English. They are in fact often omitted when in the subject position. In English we have to say '<u>who</u> went' in the sentence 'I went to Kyoto yesterday' if it is clear you are talking about yourself, in Japanese you can merely say **kinoo Kyoto e ikimashita** (yesterday to-Kyoto went). The most frequently used pronouns in Japanese are **watashi** (I) and **anata** (you); 'he', 'she' and 'they' are far more uncommon.

Adjectives Like in English, Japanese can use adjectives in two ways, before the noun they describe (**mushiatsui** hi, a **humid** day) or following it (kyoo wa **mushiatsui** desu, today is **humid**). In grammatical terms, adjectives can in fact function as verbs, and have tenses like verbs (see below).

Verbs The verb is probably the most important element in the Japanese sentence, since it is quite possible for the sentence to consist of a verb and nothing else:

tabemashita   (I, we, he, she, they, you, etc.) **ate**

Functions like tense, negation and level of politeness are shown by adding suffixes to the base form of the verb.

Whereas in English tense and agreement are probably the most important things about a verb, in Japanese the verb is the main way gradations of social status are marked. In the modern language there are three basic levels of politeness: the plain, or informal; the polite, or formal; and the honorific. If you look up a verb in the word list you will find it written in the base, or plain, form: for example, **taberu** (to eat) or **miru** (to see). This is the form used in informal conversation, so, for example, you might say to a friend 'ashita ii restoran ni **iku**' (tomorrow I'm going to a good restaurant). However, when you talk to people you have only just met or to someone senior to you, you must use the polite form, for example, 'ashita ii restoran ni **ikimasu**'. The **-masu** ending always indicates the polite level. The honorific level is used when someone wishes to show extreme politeness, either because of their own humble position (a shop assistant to a customer, for example) or because of the exalted nature of the person he or she is speaking with (like a company president). Honorific language is very complicated and even Japanese people find it difficult. In the phrasebook, the informal level has been used in close personal situations, the polite in general conversation, and the honorific only when showing how someone in a service situation might address you.

In comparison to English the form of Japanese tenses is simple. The future tense has the same form as the present, so that **tabemasu** could mean 'I eat' or 'I will eat'. The past is shown by adding the suffix **ta**: tabemashi**ta** (I ate), mimashi**ta** (I saw). The only other form used for tense is the continuative, made using the suffix **te**: tabe**te** imasu (I am eating); tabe**te** imashi**ta** (I was eating). English speakers may find the lack of a perfect tense (I have done-) confusing, but Japanese employs other, non-verb forms, to express this.

The negative is made by adding the suffix **nai** to the plain form of the verb, for example, tabenai (I do not eat), or the suffix **n** to the polite **masu** ending, for example, tabemase**n** (I do not eat).

3 Particles

Japanese is very different from English in that the relationships between the various parts of speech are shown by the use of particles. English uses word order to indicate meaning: 'the dog bit the man' and 'the man bit the dog' are different entirely because of the order in which the words come in a sentence. In Japanese the meaning is not dependent on word order but on particles; the doer of the action (subject) is shown by the particle **ga** and receiver of the action (object) is shown by the particle o:

inu **ga** hito **o** kanda (literally, the dog-the man-bit: the dog bit the man)
hito **ga** inu **o** kanda (literally, the man-the dog-bit: the man bit the dog)

Japanese has another particle, **wa**, which often marks the subject as well. This has the function of pointing out a particular word and making it stand out from the rest of the sentence as the topic.

kono seki **wa** aite imasu ka? (as for this seat, is it free: is this seat free?)

koko ni wa nani ka omoshiroi no ga arimasu ka? (as for in this place, is there anything interesting here: is there anything interesting here?)

The above examples also show the use of the question-making particle **ka**.

Another important particle is **no**, used principally to join nouns together, so functioning like the English possessive.

watashi **no** namae (literally, the name of me; my name)
igirusu **no** shimbun (literally a newspaper of England; an English newspaper)

Other particles act like English prepositions: **ni** (at, in, on, to), **e** (to a place), **de** (at, with), **kara** (from), **made** (to, until), and **yori** (from).

4 Some useful grammatical forms

The phrase book has shown you how to say things as you need them in different situations. Let us bring together some useful forms that might help you to make new sentences, using words from the wordlist.

Please do something A general imperative is the **-te kudasai (-te kuda-sigh)** ending added to a verb:

taberu (eat)	tabe**te kudasai**	please eat
miseru (show)	mise**te kudasai**	please show me
kuru (come)	ki**te kudasai**	please come
kaku (write)	kai**te kudasai**	(please write)

You can negate this with the phrase **naide kudasai (nigh-de kuda-sigh)**:

taberu	tabe**naide kudasai**	please don't eat
miseru	mise**naide kudasai**	please don't show me
kuru	ko**naide kudasai**	please don't come
kaku	kaka**naide kudasai**	please don't write

Have to do The most usual way of showing necessity is **-nakereba narimasen**:

iku	ika**nakereba narimasen**	I have to go
suru	shi**nakereba narimasen**	I have to do
miru	mi**nakereba narimasen**	I have to see

Want You can show that you want to do something by adding **-tai n(o) desu (-tigh n(o) des)** to the verb:

iku	iki**tai n desu**	I want to go
yomu	yomi**tai n desu**	I want to read
miru	mi**tai n desu**	I want to see

Please When you want someone to do something for you, say **onegai shimasu**, literally 'I beg of you'. This is a useful phrase that can be used in a variety of ways. If someone offers to do something for you, you can use it to accept:

| **biiru wa doo desu ka** | would you like some beer? |
| **Onegai shimasu** | yes, please |

If you want an item in a shop, say what it is with '**onegai shimasu**':

| **hon onegai shimasu** | a book, please |
| **pan onegai shimasu** | bread, please |

Useful verbs Two of the most useful verbs are **desu (des)**, equivalent of is/are and **arimasu (arimas)**, 'there is/are':

| watashi wa Igirisujin **desu** | I **am** English |
| aita heya wa **arimasu ka** | **are there** any vacancies? |

5 A final tip

The Japanese language is full of loan words, most of them from English. They are used to name things, and so are almost always nouns. If you get stuck for a word, try pronouncing the English word slowly in a Japanese way. For example, if you pronounce 'bus station' syllable by syllable, *ba-su su-tay-shon*, this will turn out to be a perfectly understandable Japanese word.

The Japanese writing system

Written Japanese combines three different scripts, *hiragana*, *katakana* and *kanji*. Hiragana consists of 46 syllabic characters and is used to write the grammatical elements of the Japanese sentence, like particles and verb endings. Katakana also has 46 characters, and is used to write foreign words. The meaningful component of the sentence is written with *kanji* (Chinese characters), that is, nouns, adjectives, some adverbs and the base form of verbs.

Igirisu no **hon** o **ka**imashita   I bought an English book

Igirisu will be written in katakana, being a foreign word, **hon** and **ka** in Chinese characters, and the remaining syllables in hiragana.

Place names on station notice boards will almost always be written in *kanji*, but the pronunciation in *hiragana* is also given beneath. In the large cities, the pronunciation in the latin alphabet (*romaji*, 'Roman letters') will also appear. The *kanji* give the meaning to the word. For example, To-kyo means 'eastern capital', O-saka means 'great slope', Hane-da means 'field of wings' and Roppon-gi means 'six trees'.